Aquarium fishes and plants

Aquarium fishes and plants

Text by
K. Rataj and R. Zukal

Illustrations by
J. Malý

Spring Books

Translated by
Daniela Coxon

Designed and produced by
Artia for Spring Books
Published by
The Hamlyn Publishing Group Limited
London • New York • Sydney • Toronto
Hamlyn House, Feltham, Middlesex, England
© Copyright Artia 1971
Reprinted 1972, 1973

ISBN   0 600 30056 0

Printed in Czechoslovakia by Polygrafia 3, Prague
3/01/07/51

Introduction

An aquarium can be an important decorative feature in a modern home. It can fulfil an aesthetic role as a colourful live picture, apart from contributing to a biological improvement of the atmosphere. It increases the humidity of the air so that all kinds of house plants which are grown unsuccessfully in other conditions, can flourish in centrally heated homes.

An aquarium is a part of nature but it need not be a copy. In other words, in arranging a community of plants and fishes this need not correspond to natural conditions. Bearing in mind the environmental needs of animals and plants, it is possible to breed fishes from different continents together, and even to rear tropical fishes with those from the temperate zone. But this requires a fair knowledge of biology and constant care in maintaining a suitable environment.

However, the easiest way to maintain a biological balance in the aquarium is the creation of a so-called biotopic aquarium in which fishes and plants are kept which originate in the same geographical region and have approximately the same needs. This book is arranged in accordance with such a system and individual lists show areas of aquatic life from the tropical zones of Asia, America and Africa.

Biological balance in the aquarium

Fishes and plants are an integral part of every aquarium. While plants are able to vegetate without fishes, fishes can only live without vegetation with the help of a whole range of technical aids.

Plants are producers and have an ability to build up organic material from minerals. The animals, in our case fishes, are consumers dependent for food on completed organic materials.

A suitable arrangement of fishes and plants is on the basis of biological balance. The excrement left by fishes, so-called detritus, putrefies with the help of bacteria and other microorganisms into mineral substances. The plants consume these and create from them a living substance which can be digested by the fish thus complementing their food. While the plants manage to consume excremental substances everything is in order. As soon as detritus accumulates, the biological balance becomes vitiated. The organic content in the water rises and both fishes and plants begin to die off.

Plants produce oxygen which fishes inhale. When fishes breathe, carbon dioxide is released which plants accept and which is then re-assimilated. At night it is the opposite with plants; they absorb oxygen and emanate carbon dioxide, in a similar way to fishes. But at this time the fishes are at rest, so that their consumption of oxygen is negligible. That is why a mutually positive influence exists.

The circulation of oxygen and carbon dioxide can also be regulated by an artificial complex apparatus. A system of air pumps, tubes, and filters should not be the sole source of maintaining the biological balance; it should merely supplement the natural relationship between plants and fishes when the breeder upsets this balance with breeding excessive numbers of fishes.

The most suitable and the least disturbing device is the familiar pumping in of air, which rises from the bottom in the shape of fine bubbles. Aeration oxidizes the water and mixes the lower parts of the water-level with the top, so that the temperature in the tank is even. Better still is the biological filter which is inserted under the layer of sand at the bottom of the tank. The biological filter ensures the uniform temperature of water and the bottom bed, so that the plant roots and leaves function with approximately the same intensity. Apart from this the biological filter oxidizes not only the water but also the bottom area of the tank, it helps the roots to breathe, and prevents putrefaction of the detritus which has penetrated the sand.

Nourishment of aquarium plants

Water plants are not only dependent on the nourishment received by their roots as are the majority of the surface plants. They receive nutriments over the entire surface of their bodies, starting with the skin of their leaves. Some of the typical submersed (living under water) plants do not grow roots at all *(Ceratophyllum, Utricularia)* or if so only very short ones *(Elodea, Najas)*. That is why plants not only depend on the composition of the bed but also on that of the water which itself contains many mineral substances. It is necessary to take this into account in the composition of the earth which is to form the bottom bed.

Many aquarists add various other sources of nutrition to the bed, such as mould, leaf mould, peat, and artificial fertilizer. Generally speaking, none of these ingredients are recommended. They make the bottom impenetrable, make the use of biological filters impossible, and inevitably this leads in time to anaerobic putrefaction, arising from the insufficient supply of oxygen, which leads to the formation of poisonous gases and the decay of plant roots.

In principle the bed should be made from clean, assorted, and washed sand. The sand particles should be 2—5 mms ($\frac{1}{12}$ — $\frac{1}{5}$ ins) in size; smaller grains must be separated by a suitable sieve. Remnants of food then easily sink into such sand, oxygen permeates the coarse sand, and that is why rapid mineralization of detritus takes place and a sufficient amount of nutriments for plant life is released. If the biological filter is placed under such a bed, the biological balance is largely guaranteed and the nutrition of the plants is taken care of.

It is self-evident that in an aquarium laid out in such a way, the plants have, at first (from two to five months), a deficiency of nutriments. That is why tanks are furnished with mature plants with larger rootage and rootstocks so that they have a sufficient amount of reserve materials from the initial growth period.

If in the description of individual plants the poor bed or the moderately nourished bed is mentioned, this does not mean a base without a single ingredient or with ingredients of mixed nutriments. In every case a bottom composed of clean, washed sand is implied. The bed in a newly established tank or aquarium with a small number of fishes is considered poor. Beds are medium rich to rich for between six and eight months after the foundation of an aquarium moderately or well stocked with fishes. In addition the principle is accepted that in a tank with a predominance of live-born fishes the bed is richer than for instance in tanks populated by tetras, etc.

Nourishment of aquarium fishes

In order to breed nicely coloured and disease-resistant fishes in the aquarium, attention must be paid to their nourishment. There are many views on feeding fishes, but first and foremost their natural requirements must be considered.

When fishes are bought from a pet shop, it should be ascertained whether they can be provided with the necessities of life. Predatory fishes, for example, do not accept dried food; nor can other species be fed all year round with one sort of food. Each food contains certain substances and only with a suitable variation can a proper and balanced diet for fishes be ensured.

Correct feeding is not only important for fishes but also for the cleanliness of the tank. It is therefore better to feed the fishes frequently, but only a little at a time — preferably once or twice a day and then only as much as the fishes can consume at once. One day a week do not feed them at all so that they scavenge all food remnants. Unconsumed food decays and supports the proliferation of infusoria which can lead to fish illnesses, especially in winter when the fishes are more sensitive. With the fall in the temperature of the water, digestive and secretory processes are slowed down. Therefore in winter in unheated aquaria the fishes should be fed three times a week at the most and only so much as they can consume immediately. Make sure that the fishes do not get entirely unsuitable food like pieces of bread which decay quickly in water.

Artificial food cannot be substituted for live food all the time. Carnivorous fishes should be fed all the year with live food, herbivorous fishes mostly with dry and plant food, but most of the fishes should have a mixed diet, that is, largely live food with dry food as a supplement.

The most common live foods are mudworms or riverworms *(Tubifex tubifex)*, which can be caught in river mud in places where drains are emptied. These worms are usually for sale in pet shops. Riverworms must be looked after so that they do not die from a lack of oxygen. Put them into a shallow china or glass basin into which water is continuously dripping. If you cannot do this, store the riverworms in a cold place and cover them with water so that the top part of the ball of worms sticks up out of the water which should be changed at least three times a day.

According to circumstances fishes can also be fed with whiteworms *(Enchytraeus albidus)*, which can be bred at home in wooden boxes. Next there are earthworms *(Lumbricus terrestris)*, which are suitable for all predatory fishes, especially the family Cichlidae. Larger earthworms can be killed by dipping them into boiling water. Slit them with a razor blade, wash them, and serve them to the fishes cut up. *Turbatrix aceti* are amongst the smallest food and are used for feeding fry about a week old.

The red larvae of midges *(Chironomus)* constitute very sound food. They can be caught in river mud. Give the fishes only a little of the larvae at a time, and see to it that they consume everything straightaway. Otherwise the larvae burrow into the bed where they turn into pupae and in time midges are hatched whose presence in a room is unpleasant, even thought they do not bite. The larvae of the common gnat *(Culex pipiens)* are also a first-class change in the fish diet. They can be caught from spring until late summer in small reservoirs, woods, and gardens.

Among the most common food, live or dry, are minute crustaceans, water-fleas *(Daphnia)*, and *Cyclops*. They are nearly all to be found in stagnant water where they can be netted. Microscopic plankton food for fry, such as the larvae of *Cyclops* called nauplii, various sorts of infusoria, Rotifera, etc., can all be caught with a net of appropriate density. The correct distribution of this food according to size is very important as coarser food, especially *Cyclops*, can kill the fry. Feed the fry only with food as big as the eye of a fish.

Another source of food is the brine shrimp *(Artemia salina)*. It is a small sea crustacean, growing to the size of 1 cm ($\frac{4}{10}$in.), whose tiny eggs keep for many years in dry conditions. After throwing them into salty water, nauplii hatch out. Directions for hatching will be provided by all specialist shops.

If live food is given to the fishes, it often happens that animals are introduced into the aquarium which can be dangerous to the fishes or their fry. There are for instance hydras (Hydrozoa), which multiply very quickly and then hang in whole colonies from the plants. The best known are brown hydras *(Hydra oligactis)*, common hydras *(Hydra vulgaris)*, and green hydras *(Hydra viridissima)*. If they penetrate the spawning tanks, they destroy the spawn and even several-week-old fry. They even eat some fishes, for example paradisefishes *(Macropodus)* and gouramis of the genus *Trichogaster*. Hydras can be killed with the help of special preparations. Planarians *(Planaria)* are even more dangerous and it is very difficult to destroy them. They eat food meant for the fishes and fish spawn. They secrete slime by which they cling to the walls of the aquarium, to the bottom, and to the plants. Fry can get stuck to this slime and thus be destroyed. Planarians either eat them or they simply die as they never escape from the slime. Planarians can be dangerous even to larger fishes. A fish, which is weak, sinks down to the bed or hides between the plants. If planarians are near such a weakened fish, they can literally leave it a bare skeleton by morning. Another danger is the carp louse *(Argulus foliaceus)*. With its two suckers it clings to the bodies of fishes and sucks their blood. In so doing it makes the fishes very weak. The carp louse grows to a size of up to 8 mms ($\frac{3}{10}$ in.).

Illumination of the aquarium

The time of illumination in hours is more important than the intensity of the light — this is the main and the most important principle in the illumination of aquaria.

Tropical plants are plants used to a short day. The day in the tropics lasts approximately twelve hours and tropical plants are only able to survive this length of day throughout their entire existence. The day in temperate zones is longer during the summer. Some tropical types stand up to such a daily routine well. Primarily the stem and the leaves develop (that is, the vegetative organs). The plants do not usually flower.

Subtropical plants are exposed in their native land to a variation in the length of day so that they adapt better. Twelve hours of daylight suits them. The plants of the temperate zone require for their vegetation (the formation of foliage) between eleven and fourteen hours of daylight, for flowering eleven to sixteen hours. The necessary length of time for illumination cannot be substituted by a greater intensity of light for a shorter time.

By additional lighting the prolonging of the winter day is inferred, and not the increase of the total light intensity during daylight hours. In effect it means that in winter it is necessary to prolong the daylight for plants by about four hours. Artificial lighting has to form a continuum with the daylight in the morning or in the evening and it is necessary to adhere strictly to the chosen time of artificial lighting so that the plants maintain a natural rhythm of vegetation. Plants are especially sensitive in the time after the autumn equinox when the day begins to get shorter than twelve hours.

As regards the intensity of illumination the plants which require plenty of light are known, but on the other hand a surplus of light can harm some plants. Aquatic plants are normally exposed to less light than surface plants. In dense forests the aquatic vegetation forms several layers; the final layer is often overlaid as well by coastal and floating vegetation. Apart from this, water admits much less light than air, so that the light falling on the leaves of submersed plants is naturally weakened considerably.

Amongst the relatively light-loving plants are to be found first of all representatives of the family Alismataceae *(Echinodorus, Sagittaria)* and some representatives of the family Hydrocharitaceae *(Vallisneria, Elodea, Lagarosiphon)*. Amongst the shade-loving plants are first of all representatives of the family Araceae *(Cryptocoryne, Anubias)* and others.

Fishes are not exceptionally sensitive to the length and intensity of light, although there are varieties which are most content in mildly dispersed light while other types like tanks which are, at least for a part of the day, exposed to the sun. The spawn of a whole range of aquarium fishes are rather sensitive to light. For these the tank should be darkened after spawning.

The individual demands of plants and fishes for light are mentioned in the special texts with corresponding coloured illustrations.

The temperature and heating of the aquarium

Provided the tank is restricted to fishes and plants from the temperate zone there is no need to worry about heating. The inhabitants of such an aquarium survive in winter in normal room temperatures. But the cold-water unheated aquarium is more elaborate than the tropical aquarium. The temperature in it, dependent on outside conditions, fluctuates during the year, so the microbial activity changes and very often a disorder occurs in the biological balance, clouding the water and killing the fishes and plants.

In the warm-water aquarium approximately the same conditions are maintained throughout the year by heating and by appropriate artificial lighting. So the conditions for the regular maintenance of the biological balance are provided and the tank is kept nice and tidy all the year round without undue effort.

In the mildly heated aquarium South Asiatic carp fishes can be bred, for example some species of the genera *Puntius*, *Danio*, and *Tanichthys* which require clean and pellucid, not very old water, and plenty of light. Fishes from the temperate and subtropical zones of South America also belong to this group. The temperature of water in such a tank is between 18—21°C (64—70°F).

Tanks heated between 22—28°C (72—82°F) (tropical aquaria) facilitate the largest range of gaily coloured, interesting fishes and plants. The aquaria are heated most often by electric heaters which are based on the same principle as the immersion heater. They can be connected to direct and alternating current. The voltage tension can vary. In specialist shops there are heaters with different calorific strengths. A heater is usually chosen which, when connected, raises the temperature of the water 2—4°C (4—7°F) as compared with the temperature of the environment. Depending on the capacity of the tank count 1 watt for 2 litres of water, so that for a 100 litre aquarium a 50 watt heater is necessary. The heater is usually used with an automatic thermostat. In this way not only is a completely regular temperature achieved in the tank, but also the water is prevented from getting too hot on warm days.

The correct temperature in the aquarium should not exceed 22°C (72°F) in winter and it should not drop below 18°C (64°F), especially when correct and effective artificial lighting is not installed. If the plants lack light in winter, the tank should not be heated to too high a temperature as high temperatures tend to decrease the oxygen content of water.

Cloudiness of water caused by algae

Fresh water, either surface or tap water, contains on the one hand the embryos of one-cell algae and Protozoa, and on the other hand a sufficient quantity of the minerals for their procreation. These fine organisms multiply greatly and cause the cloudiness of the water which is a common phenomenon, especially in recently established aquaria. It usually lasts between five and ten days, then disappears, and does not recur. The aquarist beginners often make the mistake of changing the water. In so doing they add new embryos and new water rich with nutriments and so they prolong the duration of the cloudiness for another five to ten days.

If the cloudiness lasts more than fourteen days, water filtration should be introduced which will remove the cloudiness but not its cause. If the excess of algae and Protozoa is caused by too rich a bed (a surplus of organic materials), the cloudiness is renewed immediately when filtering is stopped and it lasts until the surplus of nutriments in the water is used up (possibly for several months). This is another reason for having the bed made from clean sand.

The cloudiness of water in older tanks usually has a seasonal character. In summer green cloudiness most often appears, which is formed by the one-cell green algae. It is caused by a surplus or even a sufficient amount of light. This cloudiness is very beneficial for all life in the tank, but it reduces the transparency of the water and therefore it is especially unpleasant for the aquarist, as it detracts from the decorative effect of the tank. The green cloudiness is consequently a sign of a sufficient amount of light but also of a surplus of minerals in the water. As soon as the green algae consume the minerals from the water, they die altogether and their bodies enrich the water with organic materials on which the smallest animals again multiply (that is, one-cell Protozoa). The green cloudiness then changes into a grey or brown one which is no longer useful for the life in the tank, but on the contrary can be very dangerous. The Protozoa are animals and often take such a great amount of oxygen from the water that even the fishes can die.

In such cases a substantial part of the water can be changed, but it must be substituted with water from another clean aquarium or with rain water. Water from surface sources or from the tap usually does not stop the development of Protozoa. The introduction of effective filtration also helps and here the biological filter is the most effective. The filter employed must be able to clean the water in two to three days, for if it takes any longer the cloudiness of the water caused by the Protozoa can be dangerous for the life of both the fishes and the plants.

The arrangement of room aquaria

The aquarium in the home can have various purposes, but it should always give a pleasing impression. Therefore the arrangement of the bed and the installation of plants must not only satisfy the needs of plants and fishes but it should be as aesthetically perfect as possible.

The bed of the aquarium, composed of clean, washed sand, should not be flat but should be terraced and form irregular deep and shallow areas. Reinforce and decorate the aquarium bottom with small and larger stones. The most suitable are hard, indissoluble materials which do not emit materials into the water which reduce its quality. Completely unsuitable are limestone and sandstone. The material employed should be uniform to create a natural impression.

Apart from stones, old branches, parts of stems, stumps, and the bark of the cork-oak tree can be found useful for the aquarium. The wood must not be green or rotten. The best pieces are old parts of trees, which have been lying in the water tens of years, whose wood is permeated with minerals and is dark and hard. Ferns and water moss can be placed on the wood.

Room aquaria need not be a copy of nature. That is why the plants for them do not need to be chosen according to the geographical origin of the breeding fishes. However, the tank should be arranged with fishes and plants according to the conditions which can be created artificially.

The opposite of these are the biotopic aquaria. They are tanks which should represent as nearly as possible a sample of the aquatic life of certain regions. The community of plants and fishes is not chosen according to how the individual species fit decoratively together, but the tank is furnished exclusively with plants and fishes for instance from a South Asiatic tropical jungle, an African lake, or a lagoon in the river basin of the Amazon at the edge of a Brazilian virgin forest, etc. At the same time, of course, the aesthetic appearance of the aquarium should be considered as well.

The main tropical biotopes

In the separate tropical zones the natural conditions for the development of plants and fishes differ greatly. To start an aquarium, it is necessary first to get acquainted with the natural environment in which the aquarium plants and animals live. Tropical Asia, the South American tropics, and Africa will now be considered in turn.

The Indomalayan region

The Indomalayan tropics, next to the South American tropics, provide the main source of aquarium fishes and plants. First of all there is the Malay Peninsula and Indonesia, especially the largest islands (Java, Sumatra, Borneo, Celebes, and New Guinea). A great number of species come from Ceylon.

The most significant feature of this region is the absence of big rivers. In places, where paddy fields have not been laid out by the thorough drainage of the moorland, the whole countryside is covered with an impenetrable jungle with numerous small lakes, rivers, and swamps. The dry land is overgrown with thick vegetation and its relative proximity to the sea influences the almost constant yearly temperature, which oscillates from 25—27°C (77—81°F).

The predominant part of the region is very rainy and has no conspicuous dry season. The rains do not have a seasonal character and there are many permanent reservoirs in the jungle. For this reason a great number of typical submersed and amphibious plants originate here and hence fishes suitable for breeding in the aquarium.

The most typical water plants of this region are the family Araceae represented first of all by the genera *Cryptocoryne* and *Lagenandra*. The typical submersed types grow in invariably deep shady water. The amphibious species are submersed in the monsoon period and multiply during this time by root offshoots. During the fall in the river level they form emersed leaves and then flower.

In the artificial and natural canals which join the individual lakes *Limnophila*, *Ceratopteris*, *Bacopa*, etc., grow. In this region an unusual number of fish species live. In the pools with open sun-heated surfaces live numerous species of *Rasbora*, *Puntius*, *Brachydanio*, and others. In the water reaches, densely overgrown with fine-leaved and floating vegetation, and therefore relatively overshadowed, primarily live labyrinth fishes of the genera *Trichogaster*, *Betta*, etc. From here some fishes even get to the rice fields where they live in the cloudy, completely opaque water, containing a negligible amount of oxygen. That is why they develop a labyrinth, an organ which enables them to breathe oxygen from the air.

The Indomalayan plants do not have a definite period of rest, but some amphibious species are typical of the changes in vegetative growth, in flowering and in seeding.

Plants and fishes of the region therefore are amongst the most demanding; they are sensitive to a fluctuation in temperature, especially to a marked cooling of water which can be dangerous for some species even at 18°C (64°F), for others at 15°C (59°F). The best is a constant temperature of about 22—24°C (72—75°F).

The tropics of South America

First of all there is the river basin of the Amazon, which measures over 6,000,000 sq. kms (2,340,000 sq. miles) and is predominantly a plain, especially in the central and lower reaches of the river.

The South American virgin forests have the character not of swamps but rather of temporary reservoirs. The deep primeval forests are damp but completely without surface water. The surface water is concentrated in the neighbourhood of the great rivers which in the rainy season overflow their banks and flood a vast area. After the water subsides to the main river bed, a system of dead arms and pools develops, which in dry periods gradually changes into swamps or dries out completely.

The rainfall in the Amazon area reaches 2,000—2,600 mms (79—101 ins) a year and it increases up river. In the upper reaches of the river the dry spell is hardly noticeable. In the rainy season daily downpours occur which cause floods. The level of the Amazon usually rises 3—6 m (10—20 ft), but sometimes to 15 m (49 ft), and its flow damages all vegetation, so that in the river and its immediate vicinity only a negligible quantity of hardy plants grows. In the vicinity of the Amazon no trees grow, so open countryside develops where there is sunlight, and therefore also the oscillation of the temperature during the day and during the year is much greater than for instance in the jungle of southern Asia.

In the immediate vicinity of the Amazon annual plants, which multiply by seeds or spores, dominate its banks. The most interesting botanical areas are those lying 6—10 m (20—33 ft) above the river level, which are only flooded during the big floods in the rainy season. Here, after the water recedes, extensive lagoons are left, which gradually dry out although a part of the water stays there all year round. Both amphibious species of the genera *Echinodorus* and *Sagittaria* and totally submersed plants such as *Cabomba, Heteranthera, Myriophyllum*, etc., live there.

Interesting fishes are to be found only in the shore zones of the Amazon, primarily in the smaller tributaries, in the dead arms of the river, in the shallows, and in the lagoons. Only a small number of favourite aquarium fishes originate in the main body of the river, for example *Pterophyllum* and *Symphysodon*.

The character of small tributaries varies depending on whether they come from the open countryside (from the savannahs) or from the virgin forests. The water of the streams from the open countryside is quite well illuminated, and being pellucid, naturally warm. Some fine cichlids from the genera *Nanna-cara* and *Apistogramma* and from the genera *Hyphessobrycon*, *Copeina*, *Aphyocharax*, etc., are to be found here.

The small tributaries flowing out from the rainy virgin forests are full of fallen leaves and wood; they usually contain rather acid, brown-coloured, and basically colder water. Fishes from the genera *Hemigrammus*, *Nannostomus*, *Poecilo-brycon*, *Paracheirodon*, *Polycentrus*, *Lamprocheirodon*, and others live here.

The average yearly temperature of the air in the Amazon region is 25—26°C (77—79°F) and during the year temperature can fluctuate from 14—40°C (57—104°F); thus temperature variations are extreme. Therefore the South American type of water plants are very resistant and most of them can breed successfully even in unheated aquaria. The temperature of the water oscillates between 18—30°C (64—86°F); in the stagnant waters of the dead arms and lagoons, it reaches an average of 28—30°C (82—86°F); during the vegetation period and under extraordinary conditions in the shallow lagoons even as much as 40°C (104°F).

The aquatic plants and fishes of the Amazon region adapt better to temperature oscillation than the majority of plants and fishes from the tropics of southern Asia. The majority of the plants are amphibious and can be grown either under water or emersed or like plants growing in mud. The plants from this region do not have a set period for resting and if in winter they are given at least a twelve-hour day, they grow very well in the tank all year round.

Africa

From the standpoint of aquarium fishes and plants only the virgin forest, which in Africa provides several characteristic regions, is of interest. Amongst the most important are West Africa and the Congo basin. Day temperatures here oscillate between 25—36°C (77—97°F) and the average yearly rainfall reaches 2,000—4,000 mms (76—156 ins).

Aquatic vegetation is concentrated here on the one hand in the region of the big rivers, like the Congo and the Niger, and, on the other hand, in the smaller lagoons where the amphibious species primarily grow. In contrast to the tropical regions of South America and Asia the wealth of different species is indubitably smaller. Water-lilies mainly grow here, which are unsuitable for aquaria; *Pistia stratiotes* grows here in its millions like a weed. It is from this region that one of the most beautiful and rare water plants of the genus *Anubias* originates. Otherwise shore vegetations predominate here, incapable of growth under water, such as *Cyperus*.

Contrary to this there is an abundance of beautiful fishes. The lagoons are inhabited by fishes of the genera *Tillapia*, *Pelmatochromis*, *Hemichromis*, *Epiplatys*, etc. In the flowing clean waters there are a number of species of fundul, cichlid, and barb.

Tropical West Africa is characterized by relatively stable high temperatures, and that is why the fishes originating here have a particular need for a stable environment.

Tropical East Africa is also warm and damp, but it is typified by greater variations of temperature, which oscillate from 20—30°C (68—86°F). In the steppes the variation is even greater. The smaller lagoons in dry periods evaporate completely, therefore they do not have any typical water vegetation and mud plants prevail here which cannot be used in the aquarium. On the other hand these regions are the home of beautiful funduls of the genus *Nothobranchius*. The life of these fishes is very short and they die as soon as the ponds dry out. In times of drought the spawn spends its time in the dry mud. With the arrival of the rains the fry hatch out, grow up very quickly, and multiply.

Fishes from the family Cichlidae, predominantly represented by the genus *Haplochromis*, primarily live in the region of the big lakes, Tanganyika and Malawi.

These then are the natural conditions of the three basic biotopes from which the majority of aquarium fishes and plants originate. Starting with these preconditions and giving the fishes and the plants the right environment, the maintenance of an aquarium will not be difficult. A part of nature at its most exotic can be created in the home which will give constant pleasure.

PLATES

TROPICAL ASIA

Aplocheilus lineatus CUVIER ET VALENCIENNES

Asiatic Tooth-Carp

This fish belongs to the family Cyprinodontidae and comes from India and Ceylon from where it was imported in 1909.

The body of the fish is elongate, up to 10 cms (4 ins) long, the males being the larger and more colourful. Rows of green dots with a golden shimmer extend as far as the red fins. The anal fin of the male is black-edged, while the female has transverse bands on her body.

They should be bred in a large tank with neutral, soft water, furnished with rooted and floating plants, at a temperature of about 20°C (68°F). The fish itself is immobile and spends most of the day in the labyrinth of plants. It is predatory in adolescence and requires live food.

Breeding is easy. The fishes spawn on the fine leaves of the plants and in the roots of the floating plants at a temperature above 24°C (75°F). The fry require live food and mature after six months.

Cryptocoryne blassi DE WITT

This plant belongs to the family Araceae and comes from Thailand.

It is 20—35 cms (8—14 ins) high, and very decorative. The petiole is a little longer than the blade, which is rectangularly to broadly lanceolate, green to brown-green with a silky shimmer on the upper surface; on the underside it is a shiny wine-red. The blade measures on average 10 ×3.5 cms (4 ×1½ ins); the petiole is 10—15 cms (4—6 ins) long. The inflorescence terminates in a yellow, transversely corrugated blade.

For growth it requires acidic water, temperature about 20—25°C (68—77°F) and diffuse light. It is not particular as to the composition of the bed, but it cannot stand calcium salts. It multiplies slowly from root and rootstock offshoots. It is relatively rare and the majority of plants are imported.

Badis badis HAMILTON — BUCHANAN

Badis, Blue Perch

This fish belongs to the family Nandidae and comes from India from where it was imported in 1904.

The body is low and oval, up to 8 cms (3¼ ins) long, variable in colour, yellowish to brown with a green or blue sheen. The young fishes have dark stripes on their bodies. The head of the Badis is decorated with a black stripe. The female is smaller, more thick-set, the male is slim and in the spawning season has a completely dark 'wedding suit'.

The fishes should be bred in a large, densely overgrown tank with small caves constructed from stones and flower-pots with broken bottoms. They need a temperature of about 22°C (72°F), old water, and a soft bed. They usually live in shelters, do not like company, are timid, and move about very little. They require live food.

For breeding the temperature should be modulated between 26—28°C (79—82°F). During the spawning period the male embraces the female who lays only a few eggs. The mating takes place several successive times in the cave or in the flower-pot and lasts about three hours. There are usually forty to sixty spawn and because they are looked after by the male the female can be removed. The fry are hatched in about fifty hours; they are very susceptible, and require live food.

Aponogeton undulatus ROXB.

This plant is related to the family Aponogetonaceae and comes from India. The bulb is ball-shaped. The plant leaves dip into the water on a short or longer leaf-stalk. The blades of the leaves are green and measure 12—15×3—5 cms (5—6×1¼—2 ins). They are lanceolate, blunt, or converging at the base. Their edges are wavy but not crimped. The inflorescence of this *Aponogeton* forms a single spike, the perianth is white. Because of its pleasant leaves which grow only under the water, it is numbered amongst the favourite aquarium plants. But it is easily crossbred with other Asiatic species so that the plants obtained from nurseries are usually hybrids. Pure forms can be acquired only by importing directly.

It is not difficult to grow, being content with a poor bed of washed sand.

Betta splendens REGAN

Siamese Fighting Fish

This fish belongs to the family Anabantidae and comes from the East Indies, the Malay Peninsula, Laos, and Indonesia. It was imported into Europe as early as 1872.

The body is elongate, up to 6 cms (2½ ins) long with a broad, long, and sharply pointed anal fin. The male is recognizable by a massive dorsal fin which occupies the whole of the posterior part of the back. The female is smaller, with longitudinal stripes.

Siamese Fighting Fishes are equipped with a special device (a labyrinth) by which they absorb atmospheric oxygen and that is why the air in the neighbourhood should not be colder than the water. They should be kept in a medium-sized, densely overgrown tank at a temperature of 22°C (73°F). They need live food. The males have fights with each other which may end with a serious injury or the death of one of the rivals. At temperatures of about 26°C (79°F) the male builds a bubble nest on the surface. Then mating takes place under the nest in a close embrace and the spawn fall to the bottom where the male collects them in his mouth and takes them to the nest, which he looks after carefully. By the third day the fry are swimming about. They should be fed with small live food or with dried yolk.

Rotala indica KOEHNE

This plant belongs to the family Lythraceae and has its origins in the East Indies where it most often inhabits the rice fields. With the cultivation of rice it spread over a large region extending to the Caspian Sea.

The narrow lanceolate to linear leaves, usually connate, are on tall stalks 40—70 cms (16—28 ins) long. The upper side of the leaves is olive-green, the underside reddish-brown. *Rotala indica* grows very quickly in the aquarium; it has elaborate branches and forms ornate bushes.

Rotala does not have any special needs with regard to the composition of the water and the bed, and grows well in daylight and artificial light.

24

Botia macracanthus BLEEKER

Clown Loach, Tiger Botia

This fish belongs to the family Cobitidae and comes from Indonesia (Sumatra, Borneo). Aquarists have bred them since 1936.

Its body is strong, up to 30 cms (12 ins) long with a pointed head. The jaws have four pairs of barbels and are modified to collect food from the surface. The fish is deep orange with three wedge-shaped, velvet-black transverse bars. The fins are blood-red. With its beautiful colouring it is reminiscent of the coral fish.

It should be bred in a large, densely overgrown tank where it swims in a characteristic way alternately up and down. It is shy, omnivorous, needs pellucid, soft, well-oxygenated water at 24°C (75°F).

The fish has not yet been bred in captivity and its sex distinctions are unknown.

Cryptocoryne cordata GRIFFITH

This plant belongs to the family Araceae and originates in Malaya and Indonesia (Borneo and Java).

It grows up to 38 cms (15 ins) high and it is similar to *Cryptocoryne griffithii* from which it differs only by a yellow spathe tube covering the inflorescence. The leaf-stalk is usually twice as long as its blade, which is 7—8 cms (2¾—3¼ ins) long and 4—5 cms (1½—2 ins) broad, egg-shaped, on the upper side dark green, on the underside red, with green or brown stripes.

It is a typically aquatic plant. It should be grown in a shallow, slightly acid water in diffuse and not too intense light. In a surplus of light it does not develop properly. In shallow water the flower grows above the surface, in deeper water it flowers under the surface.

Brachydanio frankei MEINKEN

Golden Danio

This fish belongs to the family Cyprinidae and its origins are not exactly known. According to some sources it originates in India, according to others it is an artificial hybrid developed by crossbreeding.

The body is elongate, cylindrical, 4—5 cms ($1\frac{1}{2}$—2 ins) long, golden-yellow, decorated with irregular blue-black flecks. The male is slimmer. The fishes should be bred at a temperature of 20°C (68°F) in a medium-sized sunlit tank in large groups. They usually swim in shoals, are peaceful, sociable, and omnivorous.

Breeding is very easy. The fish spawn at 26°C (79°F) in a small tank, in normal tap water, between two and three days old. On the bottom of the tank put a fair amount of plants or pebbles, in between which the spawn fall. After spawning remove the fish. The fry hatch out in thirty-six hours, and afterwards they swim away and consume any sort of small food.

Limnophila sessiliflora (WAHL.) BLUME

This plant belongs to the family Scrophulariaceae and it can be found in the whole of tropical Asia, including islands, and in some places it penetrates even the subtropical zones. The submersed leaves are arranged in whorls of six to nine and usually measure 2—3 cms ($\frac{3}{4}$—$1\frac{1}{4}$ ins), so that the average size of the plant does not exceed 5—6 cms (2—$2\frac{1}{2}$ ins). The leaflets are digitate. The emersed part of the plant, rarely growing above the water, has a covering of fine hair; the leaves are broad, indented, and purple flowers grow in the axils.

This plant even survives low temperatures, under 20°C (68°F) and it is far more resistant than other members of the family. It grows very quickly. It requires a slightly sour environment with diffuse light. It cannot stand direct sunlight and grows well with cryptocorynes. It can be multiplied vegetatively by stem cuttings.

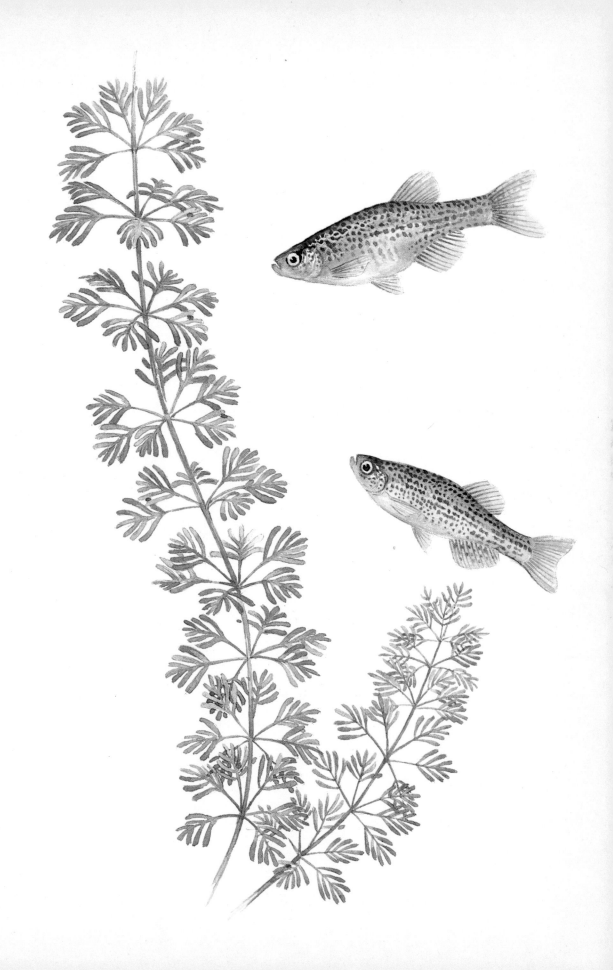

Brachydanio rerio HAMILTON — BUCHANAN

Zebra Danio

This fish belongs to the family Cyprinidae and originates in the eastern region of India, from where it was imported in 1905.

The body is slim, compressed at the sides, up to 5 cms (2 ins) long. The back is olive-green, the stomach is yellowish. The sides of the fish are decorated with typical longitudinal stripes, which extend to the caudal and anal fins.

The male is slimmer, usually longer than the female and his golden-yellow stripes are shiny. The female is more full-bodied and the golden stripes are dull.

Rearing and breeding are the same as for *B. frankei* (see previous page). These are sociable, peaceful fishes suitable for aquarist beginners.

Cryptocoryne purpurea RIDLEY

This plant belongs to the family Araceae and is derived from a region extending from India to Malaya. It grows to a height of 25—30 cms (10—12 ins). The petioles are usually longer than the blades; the blades are oval-shaped, dark green on the upper side, often dashed with brown, and on the underside purple or brick-red with darker dashes.

The blade measures 6—8 × 3.5—4.5 cms ($2\frac{3}{4}$—$3\frac{1}{4}$ × $1\frac{1}{2}$—$1\frac{3}{4}$ ins). The inflorescence grows above the surface and its length is proportional to the height of the water-level.

This plant is one of the most demanding cryptocorynes. It is very sensitive to calcium, which is the reason why it needs soft water. Direct light is harmful to it; it likes semi-shade. It multiplies slowly.

Chanda ranga HAMILTON — BUCHANAN

Indian Glassfish

This fish belongs to the family Centropomidae and comes from India, Burma, and Thailand. It was imported into Europe in 1905.

The body is deep, compressed at the sides, up to 5 cms (2 ins) long, green-yellow with a reddish shine. It is dark at the sides, with dotted bands, the fins are yellow or reddish, the dorsal and anal are lined with blue. The male is better coloured and apart from that it has a straight gas bladder, which in the female body is curved downwards. The body of the fishes has a glass-like transparency so that their skeletal framework and organs can be seen clearly.

They should be reared at a temperature of 22°C (72°F) in a medium-sized, densely overgrown, well-lit tank with conditioned, neutral, pellucid, and slightly salted water. They accept only live food, and are placid and peaceful. They are quite difficult to breed. Spawning occurs in crystal clear, neutral, and soft water, on to fine-leaved plants at a temperature of about 26°C (79°F). The fry hatch in twenty-four hours and require the tiniest live food. The difficulty of breeding lies in the fact that the fry do not chase the food, but catch it only when it passes their mouths.

Cryptocoryne costata GAGNEP.

This plant belongs to the family Araceae and comes from Vietnam, where it grows amphibiously.

The petioles are approximately the same length as the blade. The young plants have nearly stalkless leaves. The blades are lanceolate, pointed at both ends and the whole leaf measures up to 25 cms (10 ins). The upper surface of the leaves is dark, brick-red, with brown-red flecks; the lower surface is darker, often brown. But if this *Cryptocoryne* is grown with a deficiency of light, the green colour of its leaves predominates.

It grows well both emersed and under water, but it cannot stand a great fall in temperature. It is a sensitive species which roots and multiplies with difficulty, and therefore it is relatively rare. It differs in the shape and colour of its leaves from other types, and therefore it is a suitable complement to them. It requires mild to strong light.

32

Colisa labiosa DAY

Thick-lipped Gourami

This fish belongs to the family Anabantidae and originates in Burma, from where it was imported in 1904.

The body is oval, flat, up to 9 cms ($3\frac{1}{2}$ ins) long, bluish-green with irregular red transverse bars, which predominate especially at the rear. The abdominal fins are elongated in a fibrous form, red on the male's body, colourless on the female, and they serve as an organ of taste. The fishes have a special organ called a labyrinth, by which they absorb the oxygen from the air.

This species is rather timid, but peaceful and therefore suitable company for small fishes. They should be bred in a densely overgrown tank. In the spawning season the male builds a bubble nest. Spawning and breeding of the fry is the same as with *Betta splendens*.

Cryptocoryne balansae GAGNEP.

This plant belongs to the family Araceae and originates in Thailand.

It is very beautiful, growing up to 40 cms (16 ins) high, at present only used a little in aquaria. The petiole is shorter than the blade, which is narrowly lanceolate, 20—30 cms (8—12 ins) long and 1—3 cms ($\frac{1}{2}$—$1\frac{1}{4}$ ins) wide. The edges of the leaves are sharply corrugated and the whole blade is curled by fine blisters at the edges. The leaves are deep green, sometimes brownish. The inflorescence measures 10—15 cms (4—6 ins), the spathe tube is purple, spiral, and elongate like a tail.

It is not particular and can even endure hard water and plenty of light. It is also possible to grow it in direct sunshine. It multiplies from rootstock offshoots, but only very slowly. Thus the majority of the plants come from direct imports.

Colisa lalia HAMILTON — BUCHANAN

Dwarf Gourami

This fish belongs to the family Anabantidae and comes from India (Bengal, Assam), from where it was imported in 1903. It lives in poorly oxygenated water.

The body is elongate, egg-shaped, strongly compressed, up to 5 cms (2 ins) long, coloured in various shades of blue and red. There are twelve to thirteen transverse bars on the body, which are red, blue, and green. The neck is indigo blue, the eye dark red. It is one of the most beautiful and most popular fishes. The male is far more colourful than the female.

The fishes are very timid, suitable company for smaller peaceful species. They should be bred at a temperature of 22°C (72°F) in a medium-sized, well-lit tank covered with glass. For breeding purposes it is useful to place floating plants in the tank, among which the male then builds a bubble nest which is exceptionally deep in this species. The fry require small live food.

Aponogeton crispus THUNB.

This plant belongs to the family Aponogetonaceae and comes from Ceylon.

It differs from *Aponogeton undulatus* in that its leaves are longer, growing to a length of 30—50 cms (12—20 ins) and even in deep tanks reaching the surface of the water. The leaves are green, usually 2—2.5 cms ($\frac{3}{4}$—1 in.) wide. Their margins are gently curled and the waving of their edges is more pronounced than with *A. undulatus*. The inflorescence measures 10—15 cms (4—6 ins), the perianth is about 4 mms ($\frac{1}{8}$ in.) long, white, and the bulb is round.

This type requires a well-lit tank and prefers surface light. Seeds can be obtained easily from maternal plants grown from imported bulbs. Plants supplied by nurseries are usually hybrids as they crossbreed easily with each other. Imports are more sensitive — they do not hibernate well. The plants require a period of dormancy, therefore the temperature should be decreased for them to 14—15°C (57—59°F) in winter. Then they usually lose all their leaves, but in spring new ones grow quickly from the bulb, then the plants blossom prolifically and create a large number of seeds.

Danio malabaricus JERDON

Giant Danio

This fish belongs to the family Cyprinidae and comes from India and Ceylon. It was imported in 1909.

The body is slim, elongate, strongly compressed at the sides, and up to 10 cms (4 ins) long. The back is steel-blue, the flanks greenish, behind the gills there are two to three transverse golden bars, and the sides are decorated with blue and goldish longitudinal stripes. The male is usually smaller and has more distinctive colouring. In the spawning season he has orange pectoral fins.

For breeding this *Danio* needs a spacious tank with a small number of plants and a temperature about 20°C (68°F). In a small tank the fishes are timid and often jump out of the water. Otherwise they are sociable and peaceful.

For spawning they should have a sufficiently long tank with normal water at a temperature of about 26°C (79°F), plenty of finely leaved plants on the bottom or pebbles, among which the spawn fall. After spawning take the parents away. The fry hatch in thirty-six hours. After swimming away feed them with small live food.

Microsorium pteropus (BLUME) CHING.

Java Fern

This plant belongs to the cryptogamous plants of the family Polypodiaceae and originates in India, southern China, and the Indomalayan region up to the Philippines.

From the creeping rootstock the leaves grow 10—25 cms (4—10 ins) long and 3—7 cms (1¼—2¾ ins) broad. The blades are broad lanceolate, plain-edged, green to brown-green and have a striking venation. The edges of the leaves are wavy.

This is one of the most beautiful ferns. It is not particular about the composition of water and grows well in a light or semi-light place. It multiplies by shedding plantlets which grow at the edges of fully developed leaves.

It is grown by attaching it to submerged branches or stumps. Never plant it in the sand like other plants. It requires a temperature about 20—25°C (68—77°F).

Labeo bicolor H. M. SMITH

Red-tailed Black 'Shark'

This fish belongs to the family Cyprinidae and comes from Thailand. It was imported as late as 1952.

The body of the female is elongate, up to 12 cms (4¾ ins) long, completely black, only the caudal fin is blood-red, the pectoral fins are orange. In front of the snout there are two movable, forward-jutting barbels. There is another pair at the corner of the mouth. The dorsal fin is high, pennant-shaped and similar to a shark's fin. It is difficult to distinguish the male from the female.

The best environment for this *Labeo* is a large, densely overgrown, softly lit tank with pellucid, soft, slightly acidic water at 22°C (72°F). Apart from live food it also requires plant food; it eats algae and also lettuce leaves.

It is not yet certain whether the breeding of young fishes in captivity has been successful. Reputedly the female lays eggs into an overturned flower-pot at a temperature of 26°C (79°F), and the male takes care of the spawn.

Barclaya longifolia WALL.

This plant belongs to the family Nymphaeaceae and comes from Thailand and Burma.

It is the most beautiful water-lily to be found in aquaria, but unfortunately it is difficult to grow. The leaves are longish, lanceolate, heart-shaped at the base and towards the tip they slowly narrow. They are up to 30 cms (12 ins) long and 3—4 cms (1¼—1½ ins) wide. On the upper side they are shiny green or brown-green, on the underside strikingly violet-red. They are delicate, almost membranous and wavy at the edges.

The only flower opens on the surface and is reddish-purple. The seeds, which are globular with delicate prickles, form easily and soon germinate.

This plant requires slightly rich to rich soil without calcium salts, soft water, and plenty of light. It thrives best in a tank illuminated at the top. Its fine leaves are easily damaged by snails and fishes, therefore it is not suitable for densely populated tanks. It requires high temperatures, with a minimum of 20°C (68°F) and it flowers only at 30°C (86°F).

Macropodus opercularis LINNAEUS

Paradisefish

This fish belongs to the family Anabantidae and originates in Korea, southern China, Vietnam, and Taiwan. Probably it was the first general aquarium fish and it was imported into Europe as early as 1869.

The body is elongate, slightly compressed at the sides, brownish to reddish with blue-green and red transverse bars. The perpendicular fins are markedly elongate, bluish to reddish with numerous blue stripes. The male is more colourful; his fins are conspicuously elongated and in the spawning season his stomach and neck get darker, the gills are black and lined with red.

For breeding a temperature of about 18°C (64°F) is sufficient, in a small or medium-sized, moderately stocked tank with a glass top. It is not particular as to the composition of the water. These fishes are predatory and aggressive; they attack other sorts of fishes, they destroy snails and the males fight each other ruthlessly. Because of their pugnacity it is better to rear them separately. The breeding is the same as with *Betta splendens*. Paradisefishes are very prolific and their fry are easy to rear.

Vallisneria asiatica MIKI

This plant belongs to the family Hydrocharitaceae and it comes from the whole of eastern Asia and Japan.

The leaves are without petioles, green, tapering, 50—70 cms (20—28 ins) long and 5—10 mms ($\frac{1}{4}-\frac{1}{2}$ in.) wide, often slightly spiral in shape. It differs from the similar *V. spiralis* in its finely indented leaf margins and deep green harder leaves. It is bisexual; female flowers are placed on long spiral stalks, the male flowers are at the base of the plant.

It should always by planted in large groups and can be used for furnishing the back walls and corners of aquaria, where it forms thick tufts, serving as hide-aways for the fishes. It is more suitable for aquaria than other types and it is not at all particular. It can endure even a very hard water and low temperature.

42

Puntius conchonius HAMILTON — BUCHANAN

Rosy Barb, Red Barb

This fish belongs to the family Cyprinidae and originates in India (Bengal, Assam). It was imported into Europe in 1903. This barb is similar to a small carp. Its body is elongated a little, deep, compressed at the sides, up to 8 cms (3 ins) long, silver-greenish with a black, gold-lined blotch at the base of the tail. The adult male is pink to red, the fins are pinkish, the point of the dorsal fin is black. This colouring is especially noticeable at spawning time.

They should be bred in a large, light, ordinarily planted tank at temperatures above 18°C (64°F). The fishes are not demanding and suitable for beginners. They are omnivorous, sociable, and peaceful. They multiply easily in normal water at a temperature of 24°C (75°F). They spawn on the fine-leaved plants and their mating is very passionate and temperamental. After spawning remove the parents. The fry number as many as 500 individuals and hatch out in forty-eight hours. They require the usual small food.

Cryptocoryne ciliata (ROXB.) FISCH.

This plant belongs to the family Araceae and comes from India, Malaya, and Indonesia.

It differs from other cryptocorynes in appearance and extent of growth. The leaves measure up to 60 cms (24 ins), the petiole is the same length as the blade, which is fleshy, deep green, longitudinally lanceolate, and squared off at the base. The inflorescence is about 30 cms (12 ins) long, the blade is purple-red with a yellow fleck and with long fringes at the margins.

Contrary to the other cryptocorynes it needs plenty of light and stands up to direct light well. To prevent it growing out of the water grow it in clean, washed sand and half-shade. It multiplies from rootstock offshoots and creeping runners, which form at the axil point.

Puntius nigrofasciatus GÜNTHER

Purple-headed Barb, Black Ruby, Nigger Barb

This fish belongs to the family Cyprinidae and comes from southern Ceylon, from where it was imported in 1935.

The body is shorter than *P. conchonius*, yellow-grey with three or four dull, blackish, wedge-shaped bars, the head is purple. The silvery edges of the scales form shining longitudinal rows of dots on the body. The male has a more remarkable colouring, in the spawning season its lateral stripes become black; apart from that, its dorsal and ventral fins are deep black and the caudal fin is black-grey.

They should be bred in a large or medium-sized tank with plenty of plants. They love half-shade and ordinary but clean water with a temperature of about 22°C (71°F). They are peaceful, sociable, and gregarious.

Breeding takes place at 26°C (79°F) in shallow water with fine-leaved plants. During spawning the fishes press close to each other, the male throws the caudal fin across the female's back, then the fishes separate and the inseminated spawn fall to the bottom. The success of the breeding depends on a well-chosen parental pair. The fry hatch out in twenty-four to thirty-six hours and are very sensitive at first to a sudden change of water.

Cryptocoryne petchi ALSTON

This plant is a member of the family Araceae and comes from Ceylon.

The petiole is approximately as long as the blade, which is lanceolate, about 5—6 cms (2—2½ ins) long, heart-shaped at the base, with slightly wavy edges. The upper surface of the leaf is brown-green to red-green, the underside is purple-red. The inflorescence measures 7—9 cms (2¾—3½ ins) and the spathe tube is red-brown.

It is not a choosy plant, grows well even in mud, stands hard water and low temperatures better than other sorts and grows as well in the half-shade as in full light. It multiplies from rootstock offshoots.

Puntius pentazona pentazona BOULENGER

Five-banded Barb

This fish belongs to the family Cyprinidae and comes from the Malay Peninsula and Indonesia (Sumatra, Borneo). It was imported in 1911.

Its body is small, rotund, embellished with five blue-black transverse bars, which are edged with yellow. The back is brown-red, the flanks reddish, the stomach yellow. The fins are dark red, becoming lighter or colourless towards the edges. The male is usually smaller, deeper coloured and has brick-red fins.

These fishes should be bred in the same way as the Red Barb *(P. conchonius)*, although they need a temperature above 20°C (68°F). They are playful and peaceful. Breeding is also the same as with the other members of the genus *Puntius*.

Cryptocoryne bullosa ENGLER

This plant belongs to the family Araceae and comes from northern Borneo (Sarawak).

The leaves measure 20—30 cms (8—12 ins), the blade is longitudinally lanceolate, usually heart-shaped at the base, 8—12 cms ($3\frac{1}{4}$—$4\frac{3}{4}$ ins) long and 2—3.5 cms ($\frac{3}{4}$—$1\frac{1}{2}$ ins) wide. It has two to three pairs of lateral veins. The whole surface area is very blistered, membranous, green, green-brown to red-brown with a purple hue. The underside of the leaf is darker than the upper surface.

The inflorescence is short and measures only 7—10 cms ($2\frac{3}{4}$—4 ins). The spathe tube is lanceolate, purple, slightly twisted, the flower case is corrugated with purple-red dots. It seldom flowers in the aquarium. This is predominantly a submersed plant, and a most attractive novelty. This cryptocoryne has been known for a long time, but only during recent years have rich natural locations been discovered from where it is now imported. It propagates very slowly and has spread amongst aquarists only thanks to the number of imports.

Puntius tetrazona tetrazona BLEEKER

Sumatra Barb, Tiger Barb

This fish belongs to the family Cyprinidae and it comes from Thailand, Sumatra, and Borneo, from where it was imported in 1935.

The body is deep, plump, yellow-white, with a brownish to olive back, the flanks have a red-brown sheen and are decorated with four typical black bands. The dorsal and anal fins are blood-red, and the ventral fin of the male is sometimes black.

The fish is one of the most popular varieties for aquaria. It requires a medium-sized tank with a water temperature above 20°C (68°F). Tap water is sufficient, slightly hard, but pellucid. The fishes cannot stand cloudiness caused by infusoria, for then they suffer from a gill disease. The characteristic posture of the fishes is an inclined position with head downwards. They are not choosy as to food. They trouble other sorts of fishes and often bite off the edges of their fins, therefore they are not suitable company for peaceful fishes with long fins.

They procreate in the same way as the Purple-headed Barb *(P. nigrofasciatus)*.

Synnema triflora (NEES) O. KUNTZE

This plant belongs to the family Acanthaceae and originates in the Indomalayan region, where it grows as an aquatic or mud plant. The stalks are thin, rooted, and fresh green leaves connately arranged grow on them. The lower submerged leaves are divided or deeply indented and usually measure $8-10 \times 3-5$ cms ($3\frac{1}{4}-4 \times 1\frac{1}{4}-2$ ins); the upper leaves initially have a full edge, but later assume the shape of the lower leaves.

Synnema triflora should be grown in a soft to slightly hard water in diffuse light. It grows well in artificial light, but sometimes fades in direct sunshine. It requires a temperature of $20-25°C$ ($68-77°F$). It is a very beautiful aquarium plant with light green colouring. It can be multiplied very quickly from stem cuttings. If the tops are trimmed regularly, very decorative bushes result.

Rasbora heteromorpha DUNCKER

Harlequin Fish, (Red) Rasbora

This fish belongs to the family Cyprinidae and comes from the Malay Peninsula, Thailand, and Sumatra. It was imported into Europe in 1906.

The body is rather deep, compressed at the sides, greyish-silver with a red to purple sheen. On its back the fish has a typical blue-black wedge-shaped blotch, terminating at the caudal peduncle. The male has the front edge of the blotch extended downwards to the stomach.

Rasbora should be bred at a temperature of 22°C (72°F) in a medium-sized, darker tank, planted predominantly with *Cryptocoryne*, in semi-hard, slightly acid, pellucid water. It is a peaceful, sociable fish, which stands out very well in a large shoal. It is not particular as to food.

It multiplies at a temperature of 26—28°C (79—82°F) in soft water at pH 6.2—6.6. The fishes spawn on to the underside of plant leaves, with their stomachs turned upwards. After spawning remove the parents and darken the tank as ultraviolet rays could harm the spawn. The fry hatch out in twenty-four to twenty-six hours and accept fine live food.

Cryptocoryne becketii THWAITES

This plant belongs to the family Araceae. It originates in Ceylon and lives in the wild in Cuba where it was introduced.

It is the most resistant of the *Cryptocoryne* grown in aquaria. The petiole is on average 8 cms (3 ins) long; the oblong lanceolate blade measures $8 \times 2—3$ cms ($3 \times \frac{3}{4}—1\frac{1}{4}$ ins) and is heartshaped at the base. The upper surface of the leaf is brown-green to red-brown, the lower surface has a light brown or purple colour. Only its emersed part flowers and its inflorescence measures about 4 cms ($1\frac{1}{2}$ ins); the spathe tube of the flower is yellowish-green.

Cryptocoryne becketii is easy to plant. It tolerates hard water and strong light. It multiplies very quickly from rootstock offshoots, and it takes quickly after being transplanted and even in the same year it spreads prolifically. This is a very suitable species for beginners.

Tanichthys albonubes LIN-SHU-YEN

White Cloud Mountain Minnow

This fish belongs to the family Cyprinidae and comes from southern China (Canton). It reaches a length of 5 cms (2 ins). In the shape of its body it is similar to the fishes of the genus *Brachydanio*. Its back is green-brown, the sides are lighter, the stomach white. From mouth to caudal fin a red-gold shimmering band stretches, ending in a dark blotch. On the upper side the stripe is edged in red, on the underside in blue. On the fins yellow and red colours predominate. The male is slimmer and his mouth is lined with light red.

Mountain Minnows should be bred at a temperature of 18°C (64°F) in a medium-sized tank, usually filled with plants, in ordinary water. It is one of the most suitable fishes for a community tank, as it is peaceful, decorative, not particular about its food, and easily adapts to a colder environment.

Breeding takes place at a temperature of 22—24°C (72—75°F). Although the parents do not usually eat the spawn, they should be removed after mating. Spawning often does not happen all at once, but continues regularly for several days. The fry accept any food, live or dry.

Hydrilla verticillata (L.) CASP.

This plant belongs to the family Hydrocharitaceae and grows from north-eastern Europe through southern Asia and Indonesia up to China and Japan, Australia, and West Africa. It is also found in the islands of Mauritius and Madagascar.

The stalk reaches a length of several metres (over 6 ft) and foliates profusely. The leaf whorls are relatively poor and are composed of three to nine leaves. The leaves are narrowly lanceolate, 15—25 mms ($\frac{1}{2}$—1 in.) long, with serrated margins.

It can be grown in any conditions as it is not particular as to the composition of the water, bed, and temperature of its environment. It stops growing in winter at a temperature of 5—7°C (41—45°F), therefore it is green throughout the year in the room aquarium. It multiplies from stalk cuttings which root well.

Trichogaster leeri BLEEKER

Pearl or Mosaic Gourami

This fish belongs to the family Anabantidae and comes from the Malay Peninsula, Sumatra, and Borneo.

The body is deep, elongate, compressed at the sides, light grey with a silvery blue sheen. On the body and well-developed fins typical pearly shimmering flecks stand out. The male has an orange, red or purple neck, breast, and stomach, the dorsal fin is strongly elongated at the back. In the spawning season the whole of the under and front part of the body is deep red. The female's colouring is less striking.

The fishes should be bred at a temperature of 22°C (72°F) in a large, covered tank in normal water. They are sociable, peaceful, but jump when frightened. They require live food.

Spawning takes place at 24—26°C (75—79°F) in the nest, which is built by the male between the floating plants. From one spawning there are usually up to 1,000 eggs, which the male looks after. It should be removed after the fry swim away.

Aponogeton stachyosporus DE WITT

This plant belongs to the family Aponogetonaceae and comes from Malaya. The leaves grow to a length of about 40 cms (16 ins), are up to 4 cms (1½ ins) wide, and their margins are wavy to curly. Some of the leaf panels are light green, others have a green to green-brown venation, so that the leaf is an irregular mosaic and very decorative. Floating leaves seldom form in the aquarium; they are wide, oval, cut into a heart shape at the base. The inflorescence has one spike, and the perianth is white.

Aponogeton stachyosporus grows well in any conditions, requiring a temperature above 20°C (68°F), and is one of those rare plants which can stand water with a rich organic content. It is the only type of *Aponogeton* which multiplies vegetatively. Bulbs form on long stems, on which roots and leaves grow.

56

Trichogaster trichopterus trichopterus PALLAS

Three-spot Gourami

This fish belongs to the family Anabantidae and comes from Thailand, the Malay Penin-sula, and Indonesia (Sumatra). It was imported into Europe in 1896.

The body is thick-set, up to 12 cms (5 ins) long, grey to silverish-olive. At the sides are two blue-black coin-shaped flecks, of which one is in the centre of the body and the second at the root of the caudal fin. The dorsal and caudal fins are decorated with pearly flecks. The male's dorsal fin is strongly elongated and pointed.

Rearing and breeding are the same as with Pearl Gourami *(T. leeri)*.

Ceratopteris thalicroides L.

Water Sprite, Indian Fern

This plant belongs to the ferns of the family Ceratopteridaceae and is found in all the tropical regions of the world. It has submersed, floating, and emersed forms. The sub-mersed and emersed leaves are odd-numbered, while the floating forms sometimes have plain, lobed leaves. Their shape is very changeable.

Ceratopteris should be grown in half-shade and also in the light. It is usually planted in the bed and then it forms leaves up to 30 cms (12 ins) long. If it is grown as a floating plant, its leaves are considerably smaller. It requires soft water and a temperature above 20°C (68°F).

It usually propagates through plantlets, which spring from adventitious buds on the leaf margins. These plants separate and float to the surface, where they vegetate as floating forms, and these floating plants form a suitable environment for the spawning of a variety of fishes. Propagation by spores is difficult.

AMERICA

Aequidens latifrons STEINDACHNER

Blue Acara

This fish, belonging to the family Cichlidae, comes from Colombia, Panama, Venezuela, and Trinidad, and was imported into Europe in 1906.

Its body is elongate, elliptical, thick-set, up to 15 cms (6 ins) long, olive-green with a blue shimmer and five to eight black, indistinctly defined, transverse bars. In the middle of the body there is a black fleck, and the gills are decorated with blue-green dots and dashes. The male has an extended dorsal fin.

They should be bred in a large tank which should be kept absolutely clean. The bottom of the tank should be covered with pebbles and a temperature of about 20°C (68°F) maintained. Acaras are relatively peaceful fishes except at spawning time; they do not dig up the bed or damage the plants. They are voracious eaters and require live food.

They multiply at a temperature of 26°C (79°F). They usually lay their spawn on a stone, cleaned in advance, or on the tough leaves of the plants. Both parents look after the spawn. The fry hatch out in sixty to seventy hours and they are not endangered by their parents.

Echinodorus latifolius (SEUB.) RATAJ

This plant belongs to the family Alismataceae and comes from the islands of the Caribbean, Central America, and the northern part of South America (Venezuela, Guyana). Among aquarists it was formerly known under the incorrect name *E. magdalenensis*.

When submersed, rosettes of leaves are formed, 10—25 cms (4—10 ins) long and 0.5—1 cm. ($\frac{1}{4}$—$\frac{1}{2}$ in.) wide, and bright green in colour. The leaves have almost no petioles. When emersed, the plant has lanceolate leaves on distinct petioles. The white flowers are 1—1.5 cms ($\frac{1}{2}$—$\frac{3}{4}$ in.) across.

These can be grown in any well-lit water or in semi-shade. It is not a choosy plant — it even withstands low temperatures — and multiplies quickly by rootstock offshoots. Under good conditions it covers the necessary area with dense fresh green growth usually up to 10—12 cms (4—5 ins) high. In well-lit conditions the plant is smaller and in half-shade taller.

Aequidens maroni STEINDACHNER

Keyhole Cichlid

This fish is a member of the family Cichlidae and comes from Guyana and Surinam. It was imported into Europe in 1936.

The body of the fish is relatively short and deep, compressed at the sides, up to 12 cms (5 ins) long, yellow-brown with a green-blue shimmer. Below the dorsal fin there is a dark fleck lined with a yellow crescent, and from this point there is a dark stripe up to the head. The eyes and gills are darkly lined. On each fin there is a dark spot. The male is usually larger and his fins are more elongate.

These fishes are bred at a temperature of 22°C (72°F), in a large tank with ordinary neutral water. They are quiet, peaceful, sometimes timid fishes. They can be bred even in the company of smaller fishes. They are not particular about their food.

At a temperature of 26°C (79°F) they often mate even in a community tank. The spawn, resting on a stone, are carefully looked after by their parents. Using their pectoral fins they constantly drive fresh water towards the mound of spawn, weeding out the mouldy spawn which are a danger. The fry can be reared even without parental care. Initially they require fine food.

Spathiphyllum wallisii REGEL

This plant belongs to the family Araceae and comes from the northern part of South America (Colombia to Guyana).

It is a mud plant, reaching in its emersed form a height of up to 50 cms (20 ins). When grown under water it is usually smaller (about 30 cms; 12 ins). The petiole is usually longer than the blade which is bright green, 3—6 cms (1—2½ ins) wide, slightly wavy at the edges, embellished with a raised venation.

Spathiphyllum wallisii is able to stand up well to a surplus of light and even thrives at lower temperatures. It grows in a similar way to cryptocorynes. It can only be bred, when emersed, from several-years-old offshoots. It grows very slowly under water. It is even possible to grow this plant in flower-pots.

Aphyocharax rubripinnis PAPPENHEIM

Bloodfin, Red-finned Tetra

This fish is a member of the family Characidae and comes from Argentina, from the watershed of the rivers Parana and La Plata. It was imported into Europe in 1906.

The body is slim, silvery-green with dark red fins, and it grows to a length of 5 cms (2 ins). The male is slimmer and more distinctly coloured. The fishes should be bred at a temperature of 20°C (68°F) in a medium-sized, long tank. They like plenty of light, fine-leaved plants and hard water with an acidity of about pH 6.8. These fishes are not particular; they are peaceful, tolerant and best of all they like to live in shoals.

Spawning occurs at a temperature of 26°C (79°F) and is similar to the genus *Brachydanio*. The fishes are very prolific and from one spawning there can be up to 500 eggs. The fry which grow very quickly are fed with fine live food.

Echinodorus osiris RATAJ

This plant belongs to the family Alismataceae and comes from southern Brazil. One of the most beautiful aquarium plants, it was discovered only in recent years.

Its leaves measure 30—40 cms (12—16 ins), the petioles are short, the blades 20—30 cms (8—12 ins) long and 5—8 cms (2—3 ins) wide, oval, with markedly protruding veins. The leaves are green, red-green or brown-green, two or three of the youngest leaves are brown-red to a golden brown. The stalks of the flowers usually grow just above the water surface.

These plants should be grown in a spacious tank, as the diameter of one tuft is 20—40 cms (8—16 ins). They require medium-hard water, neutral or slightly acidic with an established bed. They grow best at temperatures of about 20°C (68°F), but can easily endure very low temperatures. The leaves are most colourful in cold water. *Echinodorus* multiplies by casting off its offshoots or by forming young plants within the circle of its inflorescence.

Apistogramma ramirezi MYERS ET HARRY

Ramirez' Dwarf Cichlid

This fish belongs to the family Cichlidae and comes from Venezuela, from where it was imported in 1948.

It is a beautiful, rainbow-coloured fish up to 5 cms (2 ins) long. Its basic body colours change according to its mood and environment from blue to red to black with intermediate shades of purple and greenish-yellow. Along the body there is a broken band made up of six dark short stripes. The male is recognizable by the extended second spine of the dorsal fin. The fishes should be bred at a temperature of 22°C (72°F) in a medium-sized, densely overgrown tank, with plenty of light, in soft and slightly alkaline water. They are friendly and only become disturbed in the spawning season when they dig up the bed. In unclean conditions they often become ill.

Spawning occurs at 26°C (79°F), when the female lays 100—200 eggs on a stone or in hollows in the sand. The pair carefully look after the spawn, fanning clean water towards it and removing mouldy spawn. This parental care can be substituted by an aeration device situated near the heap of spawn. The fry are very sensitive to changes of temperature and unclean water.

Echinodorus parviflorus RATAJ

This plant belongs to the family Alismataceae and comes from Peru and Venezuela. Aquarists know it under the incorrect name, *E. peruensis*.

The plant grows two types of leaves on short petioles. Their blades are either long and wide lanceolate, narrowing on both sides, or distinctly heart-shaped at the base. The leaves grow to a height of 20—25 cms (8—10 ins). They are green, with a strikingly dark red-brown venation.

E. parviflorus should be planted in an old bed, in a large or medium-sized tank with neutral, slightly alkaline or acidic water. It multiplies by dividing away offshoots or by creating young plants within the inflorescent circle. The flower-stalk usually does not grow above water and young plants are then created instead of buds.

Cheirodon (Lamprocheirodon) axelrodi L. P. SCHULZ

Cardinal Tetra

This fish belongs to the family Characidae and comes from the region of the river Rio Negro, from where it was imported in 1956.

The body is elongate, about 5 cms (2 ins) long. There is a red stripe through the whole bottom half of the body, above which another, blue-green, iridescent band is situated. The male is recognizable only by his slimmer body.

Spawning occurs at a temperature of about 28°C (82°F) in a medium-sized tank without sand, but having dense tufts of fine-leaved plants and with the bottom covered by soaked peat. The water must be soft with an acidity of pH 6. It is recommended to use distilled water, acidified by peat. Never put the tank in the light. After spawning remove the parents and darken the tank.

Alternanthera rubra HORT.

This plant belongs to the family Amaranthaceae and comes from tropical South America.

This species has not yet been defined by specialists. On the upright stalk there are connate, narrowly lanceolate leaves, 2—3 cms ($\frac{3}{4}$—$1\frac{1}{4}$ ins) long and about 1 cm. ($\frac{1}{2}$ in.) wide. They are ruby-red to brown-red and very decorative.

The plant develops very slowly under water and after two to six months often dies. That is why it is principally propagated emersed. Because of the extraordinarily beautiful colouring of its leaves it pays to replace the aquarium specimen now and then by well-developed plants grown in a mud form or bought in specialist shops.

Cichlasoma festivum HECKEL

Barred or Flag Cichlid

This fish belongs to the family Cichlidae and comes from Guyana. It was imported into Europe in 1908.

The body is deep, cylindrical, compressed at the sides, up to 15 cms (6 ins) long, yellowish-grey or greenish-yellow. A broad black stripe runs obliquely upwards from the mouth across the eye, terminating in the dorsal fin. The caudal peduncle is decorated with a large, black, golden-rimmed blotch. The adult male is larger and has more pointed dorsal and anal fins.

Breeding is the same as with other cichlids. The fishes cannot stand uncleanliness and accept animal and vegetable food. They jump with fright and are therefore only suitable company for other quiet fishes.

They multiply at a temperature of 26°C (79°F). The parents look after the spawn and the hatched fry as well, but it is possible to rear the spawn using fine aeration, which can replace parental care. The fry grow very quickly.

Heteranthera zosterifolia MART.

This plant belongs to the family Pontederiaceae and comes from the whole tropical region of South America.

The stalk is thin, with a medium number of branches, very fragile, and reaches a length of 30—40 cms (12—16 ins). The alternating leaves are narrowly lanceolate, 2—4 cms ($\frac{3}{4}$—$1\frac{1}{2}$ ins) long, green on the upper side, red-brown or grey-green on the underside. The flowers are blue, but in fact it rarely flowers in the tank.

It requires soft water, plenty of diffuse light and a temperature above 20°C (68°F). The stalks and the leaves are very fine and the snails and fishes can easily damage them. To acquire richly branched bushes, the tops of the plants should be trimmed and forced to branch profusely. The plant is propagated by rooting stem cuttings.

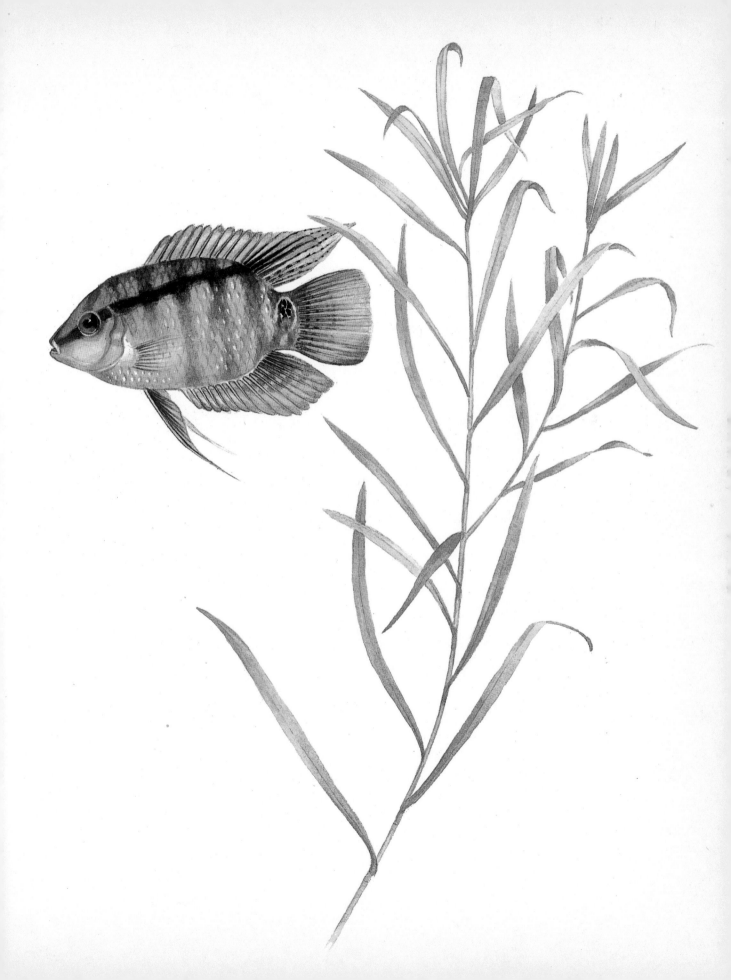

Cichlasoma meeki BRIND

Fire-mouth Cichlid, Red-breasted Cichlid

This fish belongs to the family Cichlidae and comes from Guatemala and northern Yucatan. It was imported into Europe in 1937.

The body of the fish is stout, rather deep, up to 10 cms (4 ins) long, bluish-grey with a violet sheen, and each scale is edged with red. On the flanks a dark, transversely striped pattern predominates. The bottom part of the gills has a greenish, golden-lined fleck The male is distinguished by his red neck and breast; his dorsal and anal fins are markedly elongated.

These fishes should be bred in a large tank at 22°C (73°F). They are tolerant, unparticular and usually do not dig up the bed. They require plenty of live food. They spawn at 26°C (79°F) on to the firm bed, sometimes in caves, where the female lays her eggs with her stomach turned upwards. The spotted fry hatch out in forty-eight to sixty hours, after which the parents look after them with extraordinary care.

Myriophyllum brasiliense CAMBESS.

This plant belongs to the family Haloragidaceae and comes from the southern states of the U.S.A., all Central and South America.

The submersed leaves are arranged in whorls with four to six parts; they are light to deep green. This is the only type of aquarium plant which commonly grows above the surface. The emersed leaves are shorter and tough with a velvet shine. The stalks, which grow from the tank, overhang its edges slightly.

Myriophyllum brasiliense requires a light tank with neutral to slightly alkaline water, 25°C (77°F) in summer, 15—20°C (59—68°F) being sufficient in winter. It is propagated by rooting stem cuttings.

Cichlasoma nigrofasciatum GÜNTHER

Zebra or Convict Cichlid

This fish belongs to the family Cichlidae and comes from Guatemala, El Salvador, Costa Rica, and Panama. It was imported in 1939.

The body is robust, up to 10 cms (4 ins) long, silvery grey, decorated with eight to nine dark bars. The fins are greenish with a metallic glint; the anal and dorsal fins are bordered with red. The male has longer fins while the female during the breeding season is darker with deep black bars.

Rearing and breeding is the same as with *Cichlasoma meeki*. These fishes eat ordinary food, but also algae and oat-flakes. The parents look after the spawn and the fry very carefully.

Bacopa amplexicaulis (MICHX.) WETTST.

Waterweed

This plant belongs to the family Scrophulariaceae and comes from the southern parts of the U.S.A. and Central America.

The emersed plants are creepers, with thin hair, and the flowers are dark blue. The plants grown under water are bald and green, and have darker distinct veins on the leaves which are often moderately wavy. The stalk partly lies under water, so that in good conditions this plant will spread over a considerable part of the aquarium in a short time. It is a very decorative, relatively little cultivated plant. It requires mildly acidic water. Under water it cannot stand direct sunshine and it thrives best in shady tanks in the company of cryptocorynes.

It is propagated by rooting stem cuttings. Under water it can be shaped by trimming the top. The plant then branches out strongly from the axil buds and forms very decorative bushes.

74

Corydoras paleatus JENYNS

Peppered Corydoras

This fish belongs to the family Callichthyidae and comes from south-eastern Brazil and the watershed of the river La Plata in Argentina. It was imported in 1878.

The body is cone-shaped, about 7 cms (3 ins) long, brown with a greenish shimmer and a darker pattern. On its flanks there are two longitudinal overlapping rows of bony scutes. The peculiarity of this fish is that it is not solely dependent on the water for oxygen for it has in the rear part of its gut a supplementary breathing device by which it can accept oxygen from the air. The male is smaller and has a longer, more pointed dorsal fin than the female.

These fishes are bred at a temperature of 18°C (65°F) in a medium-sized tank in any water. They collect food from the bottom. They are peaceful but stir up the mud from the bed.

The fishes spawn at 24°C (75°F), most often in a community tank in completely clean water. Two or three males are put with every female at mating time. The male draws near to the female who lays her spawn in its closed ventral fins and then she attaches them to the glass or a stone. At the point of mating the males interchange. The fry hatch out in six days and require aeration with an occasional change of water.

Echinodorus maior (MICHELI) RATAJ

This plant belongs to the family Alismataceae and comes from the Goias state in Brazil. It is known to aquarists under the incorrect name, *E. martii*.

This plant measures 30—50 cms (12—20 ins). The leaves are light green with even lighter veins; the petiole is usually very short. The blade measures $20-40\times2-7$ cms ($8-16\times1-3$ ins). In semi-shade the leaves are narrower, in full light wider.

E. maior is one of the finest aquarium plants. It should be grown in a spacious tank with soft to medium-hard water at temperatures above 20°C (68°F). It requires an established bed with clean water. It multiplies with difficulty as young plants form very rarely on the inflorescence. It can be propagated most easily from mature offshoots of older plants, so the majority of the plants are therefore imported.

Elassoma evergladei JORDAN

Dwarf or Pygmy Sunfish

This fish is a member of the family Centrarchidae and it comes from the U.S.A. (North and South Carolina, Georgia, and Florida). It was imported into Europe in 1925.

The body is about 3.5 cms (1½ ins) long, and flattened at the sides. The female is fuller than the male. The basic colouring is yellow-brown to black-brown, but the male is black at spawning time or when aroused glistening green flecks appear on its sides. The fishes are bred at 18°C (64°F), in a small densely populated tank which does not need to be heated in winter. The Dwarf Sunfishes are solitary fishes for in the company of others they go beserk and hide. In a shoal the van is led by the strongest male.

They spawn from February to April at 20—25°C (68—77°F) on to fine-leaved plants. The spawn and the fry are not endangered by their parents. The fry are fed with fine live food.

Peplis diandra (D. C.) ELL.

This plant is a member of the family Lythraceae and comes from the U.S.A. from the states of the temperate zone down to Texas, Florida, and Mexico.

It is an aquatic or mud-loving plant with a densely foliated stalk. When the plant is emersed the stem is a creeper; it floats in water. Its green fernlike leaves are so thick that the stem is reminiscent of a spruce branch. The leaves are 1.5—2.5 cms (½—1 in.) long. The stalkless reddish flowers form regularly even under water.

This plant is among the most beautiful and unusual grown in aquaria. It should be grown in a soft to medium-hard water and although it requires plenty of light, artificial light can be sufficient. It is not sensitive to temperature changes but grows relatively slowly. The freshly cut stem sections sometimes root with difficulty and after replanting they require rest. *Peplis diandra* thrives best in a tank with quiet fishes which do not stir up the bed.

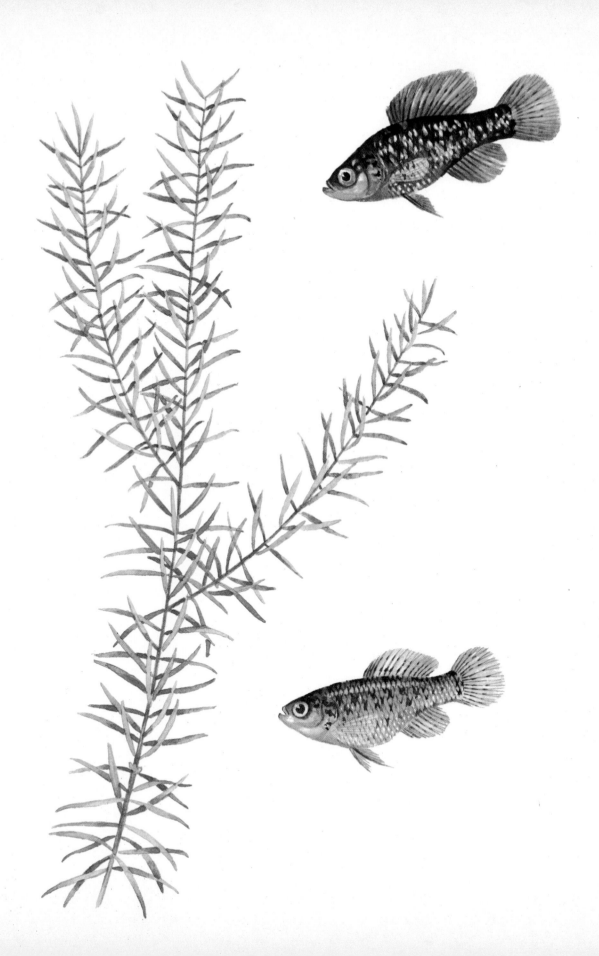

Gymnocorymbus ternetzi JORDAN

Black Tetra, Blackamoor, Petticoat fish

This fish belongs to the family Characidae and comes from the southern parts of Brazil, Bolivia and Argentina, from the watershed of the Rio Paraguay, Rio Negro, and Rio Guapore. It was imported into Europe in 1935.

The body of this tetra is deep, well flattened, and up to 5 cms (2 ins) long. The front part is silver-grey with two black bars behind the gills; the hinder part of the body is black in young fishes, but grey in older fishes. The fins are well developed. The male is smaller and thinner than the female.

These fishes require a medium-sized tank with water at 22°C (72°F). They are peaceful, like living in groups, and are omnivorous. A medium-sized tank, placed in a dim corner, is best for breeding. The water should be 26°C (79°F); semi-hard or rain water is the best. The spawn, which number up to 1,000, are laid by the Black Tetra on to fine-leaved plants. The fry swim away in six or seven days and because of their great number it is usual to divide them into several tanks.

Echinodorus horemani RATAJ

This plant belongs to the family Alismataceae and comes from the southern-most states of Brazil. It is one of the most beautiful rarities of recent years.

The leaves are up to 40 cms (16 ins) long, with the blades twice as long as the petioles and measuring $20-30 \times 4-7$ cms ($8-12 \times 1\frac{1}{2}-3$ ins). The surface of the blade is olive-green to green with a distinct silky sheen. The veins are usually lighter and very prominent. The margins of the leaves are wavy.

Echinodorus horemani is grown in an established bed in clean, medium-hard or soft water. It is not particular about temperature and can endure temperatures from 15—30°C (59—86°F). The inflorescence at present is unknown and consequently little is known about its propagation.

Hemigrammus erythrozonus DURBIN

Glowlight Tetra

This fish belongs to the family Characidae and comes from Guyana. It was imported into Europe in 1939.

The body is fragile, thin, and almost transparent. The back is an olive-yellow-green colour and from the gills to the root of the tail there is a broad gleaming ruby stripe. The length of the body is about 5 cms (2 ins). The male is slimmer than the female.

These fishes are usually bred at a temperature of 22°C (72°F). They are not particular as to the size of the tank, the composition of the water, or the environment and food. They are ideal fishes as companions for smaller tetras and barbs.

Procreation is successful in a small tank at a temperature of 24°C (75°F) in normal, not too hard, acidic water. During spawning the fishes press up to each other and in a quick movement they turn together with their stomachs upwards. At this point the female lays five to fifteen eggs. This process is repeated several times. The fry hatch out in about twenty-four hours and after swimming away require fine food.

Elodea densa (PLANCH.) CASP.

This plant belongs to the family Hydrocharitaceae and comes from a vast region, stretching from the southern states of the U.S.A. down to Argentina.

The stem reaches a length of several metres (6 ft) and branches out in a forked shape. It usually roots at the point of branching. The leaves are arranged in whorls with five segments; they are light green, 20—30 mms ($\frac{3}{4}$—$1\frac{1}{4}$ ins) long, the edges delicately serrated. It rarely flowers.

Elodea densa requires plenty of light and can stand extreme changes in temperature. It is completely indifferent as to the water, and does not even mind very hard water which it manages to soften after a time by systematic removal of the calcium salts. It can be grown rooted or freely floating in the water. It multiplies by rooting segments of the stem.

82

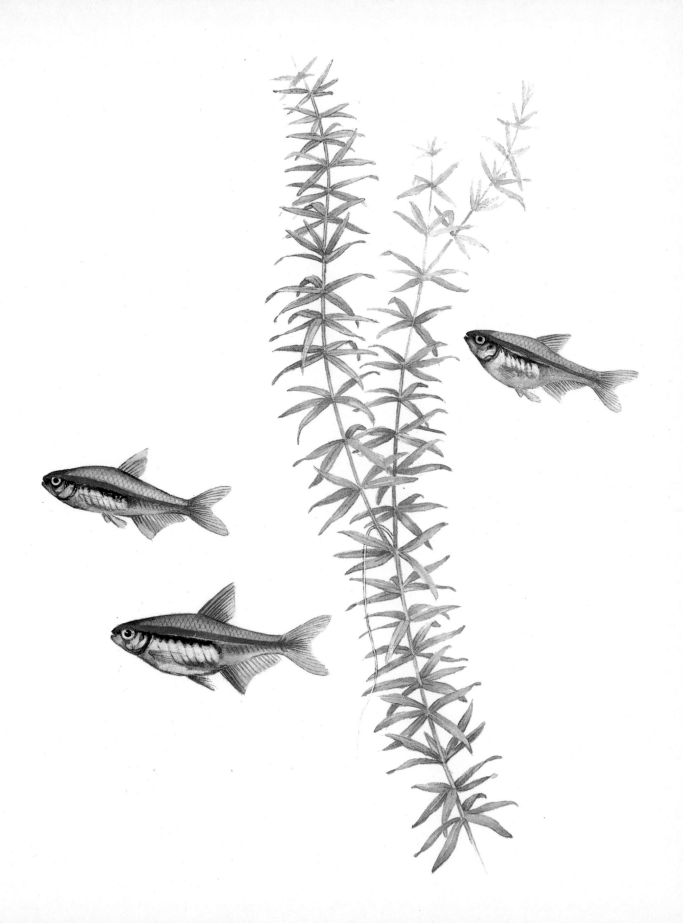

Hemigrammus pulcher LADIGES

Pretty Tetra

This fish belongs to the family Characidae and comes from the Peruvian region of the upper reaches of the Amazon. It was imported in 1938.

The body is deep, compressed, greenish, up to 5 cms (2 ins) long. The fish has on its neck several shiny patches and behind the gills there is a glistening red fleck. On the caudal peduncle is a wedge-shaped, deep red blotch, embellished by a shining gold bar. The majority of its fins are reddish. The male is slimmer than the female.

They are bred in normal aquarium conditions. They are not particular, and suitable for community tanks. The fishes spawn at 26°C (79°F) on to delicate-leaved plants in soft, slightly acidic water. After spawning the pair should be removed and the tank darkened. The fry grow very slowly, they are timid and look for the most shady places of the tank.

Echinodorus horizontalis RATAJ

This plant belongs to the family Alismataceae and comes from the Amazon watershed, from Peru and Colombia to eastern Brazil.

The leaves are 30—40 cms (12—16 ins) long. The blades measure on average 10×5 cms (4×2 ins). They are distinctly heart-shaped at the base, while on the upper surface they are very long and pointed and obtusely angled away from the petiole so that they nearly lie horizontally. The flower stalk usually grows out of the water. The flowers are white.

E. horizontalis should be grown in a well-lit tank with an established bed in soft water. It grows well both under water and emersed. It requires temperatures of between 20—25°C (68°—77°F). It is propagated from young plants which develop with the flowers within the circle of inflorescence. After ripening, the fruit are completely covered by a broad calyx, but the seeds do not usually germinate.

Hyphessobrycon callistus callistus DURBIN
Blood Characin

This fish is a member of the family Characidae and comes from the lower reaches of the Amazon, from the Para and Bahia states. It was imported into Europe in 1931.

The body is elongate, oval, flattened at the sides, about 4 cms ($1\frac{1}{2}$ ins) long, greenish, the trunk and the back are often blood-red. Behind the gills there is a distinct black dotted fleck, on the dorsal fin there is a large black fleck, and the anal fin too is bordered with black. The male is slimmer and more brightly coloured.

The fishes should be bred in a medium-sized tank at temperatures of about 20°C (68°F). They love pellucid, semi-hard, slightly acidic water and a well-lit environment. They are sociable, not choosy and require live food. They are bred at a temperature of 26°C (79°F). The rearing of the young is the same as with *Hemigrammus pulcher*.

Echinodorus pellucidus RATAJ

This plant belongs to the family Alismataceae and comes from southern Brazil. The leaves at their maximum are 25 cms (10 ins) long, the blades measuring $10-12 \times 4-5$ cms ($4-5 \times 1\frac{1}{2}-2$ ins). They are dark green with a distinctive darker venation. The young leaves often have colourful, red-brown flecks. In the aquarium *Echinodorus pellucidus* never grows out of the water. It is a very decorative and unusual plant, imported in recent years.

It should be grown in an established bed, in clean, medium-hard water. It can endure extremes of temperature and is very resistant.

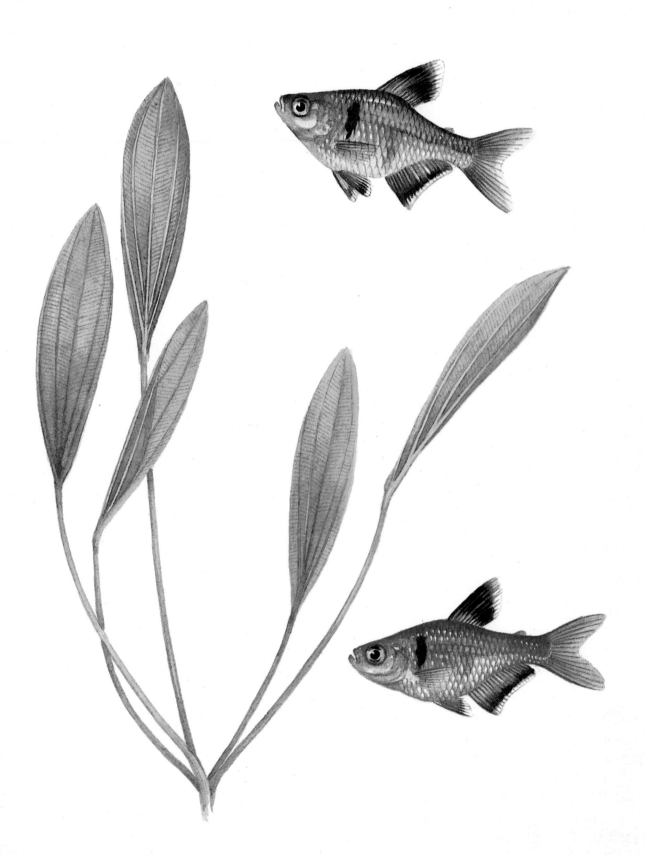

Hyphessobrycon flammeus MYERS

Flame Tetra, Red Tetra from Rio

This fish belongs to the family Characidae and comes from the environs of Rio de Janeiro in Brazil. It was imported into Europe in 1920.

The body is elongate, slightly compressed, transparent, about 4 cms ($1\frac{1}{2}$ ins) long and shiny grey in colour. Its sides are bronze to red, and its back is brilliant red as are the majority of its fins. The anal fin has a black leading edge and tip. The male is smaller and its anal fin is distinctly edged with black.

These fishes are content in a small tank and with a temperature of about 18°C (64°F). They can even endure colder water. They love the half-shade and a well-stocked tank. They are sociable, peaceful fishes, very suitable for beginners.

Hyphessobrycon flammeus procreates easily at 24°C (75°F) in a small tank with stale water. The fry spend most of their time at first near the bottom and require fine food.

Samolus valerandi L.

This plant belongs to the family Primulaceae and comes from the fresh and brackish waters of all continents. The most suitable types come from the Southern Hemisphere.

The plant creates rosettes of fresh-green, egg-shaped leaves, which narrow at the base into a short petiole. They are full-edged with prominent veins, about 6—9 cms ($2\frac{1}{2}$—$3\frac{1}{2}$ ins) long. From these rosettes now and then emerges a sparsely leafed stem, about 20 cms (8 ins) high.

Samolus valerandi requires a medium, established bed, soft water, and plenty of light. Daylight is better than artificial light. In winter it survives only if it has sufficient lighting. A slight salting of the water is useful for it.

It is propagated very easily from seeds which can only be acquired from emersed plants. If the plants form a stem under water, the segments of this can be rooted as another means of propagation.

88

Hyphessobrycon heterorhabdus ULREY

Flag Tetra

This fish belongs to the family Characidae and comes from the watershed of the lower reaches of the Amazon and from Guyana. It was imported into Europe in 1910.

The body is cylindrical, up to 5 cms (2 ins) long, and brownish. From the gills to the root of the tail there is a broad tri-coloured band composed of red, white, and black stripes. The male has a transparent cavity on its back.

These fishes are bred at a temperature of 22°C (72°F). They are lively, peaceful fishes, suitable company for other tetras. They spawn in the same way as other tetras but not always easily. They require a temperature of about 26°C (79°F), soft water, and a completely clean environment. The fry are very sensitive to being removed.

Cabomba caroliniana A. GRAY

This plant is a member of the family Cabombaceae and comes from a large region extending from the southern states of the U.S.A. to nearly all South America.

It forms a weak stem, reaching 3 m (10 ft) or more in height, on which the leaves grow, composed of numerous leaflets, 3—4 cms (1—1½ ins) long. These leaflets are wider than those of the other types of the genus *Cabomba*. Spiky floating leaves only rarely appear on the plant. The plant has white flowers.

Cabomba caroliniana thrives best in stale water, in a medium to well-lit tank without snails and numerous fishes. The stems are very fragile and are easily damaged. It requires a normal aquarium temperature of about 20°C (68°F). It is propagated by top cuttings which root easily.

Hyphessobrycon rubrostigma HOEDEMAN

Red-spotted Tetra

This fish belongs to the family Characidae and comes from Colombia. It is similar to *H. ornatus* but is larger in size. The body is brown-red with a violet shine. Behind the head at the sides there is a distinct red, pearl-bordered blotch up to 3—4 cms (1—1½ ins). The upper part of the iris is blood-red, the lower part white. There is a black stripe across the middle of the eye. The dorsal fin of the male is marked by a sickle-shaped line. The female's red blotch behind the gills is of a deeper shade.

Red-spotted Tetras are bred at a temperature of 20—22°C (68—72°F) in a medium-sized tank. They are sociable and not choosy about the composition of the water or their food. Procreation is difficult. They spawn on fine-leaved plants in a soft, slightly acid water at a temperature of 24—26°C (75—79°F).

Alternanthera lilacina HORT.

This plant belongs to the family Amaranthaceae and comes from tropical South America.

This species was imported several years ago, but it has still not been defined by specialists, and it is therefore given its trade name here. On the upright stem there are connate, egg-shaped, lanceolate leaves, measuring 4—5×1—1.5 cms (1½—2×½—¾ ins). On the upper surface they are red-green to red-brown, on the lower surface deep wine-red to dark purple. It is a very attractive aquarium plant.

Grown in soft water at a temperature of 20—25°C (68—77°F), it can stand the light and the half-shade. If its main axis is trimmed, the plant branches out luxuriantly and forms a decorative colourful bush. It is propagated by stem cuttings, which root best in spring.

Jordanella floridae GOODE ET BEAN

American Flag-fish

This fish belongs to the family Cyprinodontidae and comes from Florida and Yucatan. It has been known in Europe since 1914.

The stocky body is relatively deep, compressed, olive to brown-green. The sides of the fish are decorated with green iridescent flecks, while on the fins there are reddish spots. The female is smaller, yellowish, with a distinct fleck at the sides and her body is covered with flecks arranged in a chess-board pattern.

They should be bred apart from other fishes in a medium-sized tank at a temperature of 18°C (65°F). They are not particular, and like to eat plants and algae. They love plenty of light, but are sometimes quarrelsome. They procreate in normal water and spawn at a temperature of 25°C (77°F) on to the fine-leaved plants. After several days of spawning the female is removed, while the male looks after the spawn.

Echinodorus cordifolius (L.) GRISEB.

This plant belongs to the family Alismataceae and comes from the southern states of the U.S.A., although it also appears in Mexico. It is one of a small number of species of this genus which reaches the borders of the temperate zone. Only a few leaves, 40—70 cms (16—28 ins) long, grow from the offshoot. The petiole is longer than the blade which measures 15—20×10—15 cms (6—8×4—6 ins), is egg-shaped, and fresh-green in colour. The flower stalk is single, drooping and has white flowers measuring 2—2.5 cms ($\frac{3}{4}$—1 in.) and with them within the circle of inflorescence new plants develop, which root quickly.

The plant should be grown in indirect light in a tank with a poor bed to prevent the leaves growing above the water. It can endure extremes of temperature from 15—30°C (59—86°F). It multiplies usually by young plants growing within the inflorescence, or from seeds, which form very easily.

94

Mesogonistius chaetodon BAIRD

Black-banded Sunfish

This fish belongs to the family Centrachidae and comes from the north-eastern states of the U.S.A. (New York, Maryland). It has been known in Europe for a relatively long time, since 1897.

The body of this sunfish is short and deep, oval, compressed, silvery grey-yellow, up to 10 cms (4 ins) long. At the sides there are distinct dark stripes which, when the fins are erect, are reminiscent of a disc. The fins are embellished with darkish flecks. The whole body has a pearly sheen. The male is usually smaller, the female has a distinct fleck on the gills in the spawning season.

They are bred in a colder environment at a temperature of 18°C (65°F) and below, in pellucid stale water. They love a densely planted, not too well lit tank and they are suitable company for quiet fishes. They prefer live food.

They multiply at a temperature of 22°C (72°F). The female lays yellowish spawn in holes made by the male. After spawning the female should be removed. The male looks after the spawn and during this time he does not accept any food.

Ludwigia natans ELLIOT

False Loosestrife

This plant belongs to the family Oenotheraceae and comes from the southern parts of North America.

The connate leaves are widely lanceolate to egg-shaped, the upper surface dark shiny green, the underside brown-red or purple. The leaves measure $2-3 \times 1.5-2$ cms ($\frac{3}{4}-1\frac{1}{4} \times \times \frac{1}{2}-\frac{3}{4}$ in.). Their veins are indistinct. The fine yellow flowers grow at the axil point of the leaves only on the emersely grown plants.

This plant should be grown in a light place at a temperature from $18-28$°C ($65-83$°F). It is suitable for both cold-water and tropical aquaria.

It is propagated from top cuttings which, in suitable conditions, easily root and form colourful picturesque shrubs.

Nematobrycon palmeri EIGENMANN

Emperor Tetra

This fish of the family Characidae comes from Colombia from where it was imported in 1960.

The body is extended, slim, well flattened, up to 6 cms (2½ ins) long. From its eye to its forked tail there is a black line, superimposed with a blue stripe. The sickle-shaped dorsal fin, pectoral and caudal fins are yellowish. The male is larger than the female and his dorsal and anal fins are longer. The Emperor Tetra should be bred like other rarer tetra fish.

Fine-leaved plants are used for spawning, usually *Utricularia* or *Charra*. Before spawning the parents should be kept apart for a few days and then put in the spawning tank in the evening when it is dark. The number of spawn is small. After spawning disinfect the water with trypaflavin to prevent the spawn from being infected by mould, bacteria, etc.

Echinodorus macrophyllus (KUNTH) MICHELI

This plant belongs to the family Alismataceae and comes from eastern Brazil, from where it extends to the temperate zone of the Argentine. It is usually called incorrectly *E. grandiflorus* or *E. muricatus* by aquarists.

The leaves are 30—40 cms (12—16 ins) long. The heart-shaped blades are dark green, sometimes flecked with red-brown. They measure 20×15—20 cms (8×6—8 ins) and usually have slightly wavy margins.

E. macrophyllus should be grown in clean water with an inferior bed in a spacious tank. It is not particular as to temperature and can survive in both tropical and cold-water aquaria. It propagates by dividing its rhizomes or through young plants, developed within the inflorescence. It rarely flowers in the aquarium therefore propagation by seed is uncommon.

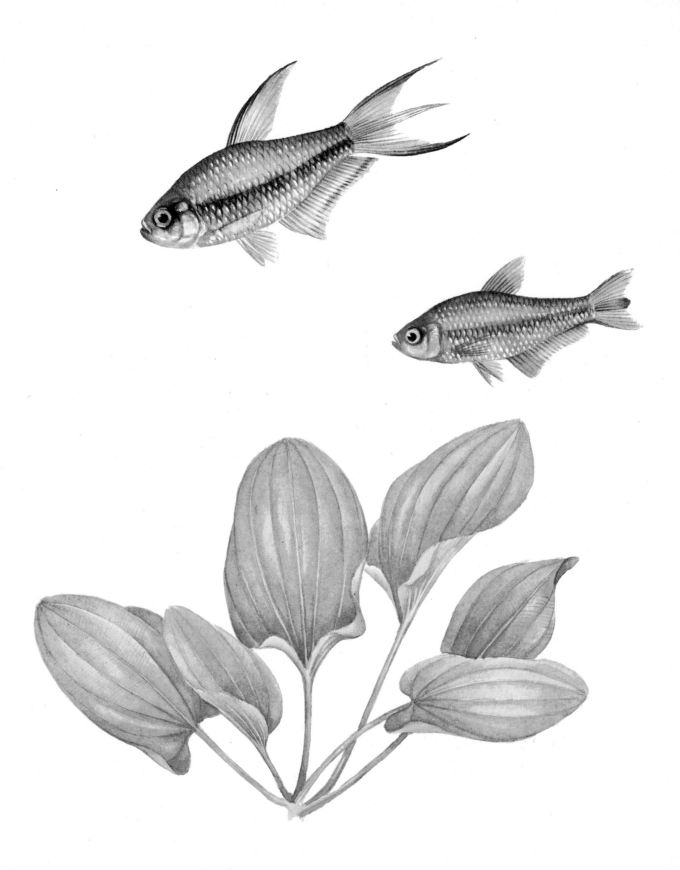

Poecilia (Lebistes) reticulata PETERS

Guppy, Millions Fish

These are live-born fishes belonging to the family Poeciliidae. They come from the northern part of South America and from the Antilles, and were imported into Europe as early as 1907.

A description of these fishes is practically impossible as they have acquired a numerous variety of forms through breeding. The males are not only very variably coloured but they also differ in the shape of fins and size of body. The most prized characteristic lies in a pure descent when the female bears homogenous offspring with the same colouring and shape of fins. The range of forms have different names. The female differs from the male usually in its larger size and its indistinct olive-grey colouring.

These fishes should be bred at a temperature of about 20°C (68°F). They are completely unparticular, peaceful and sociable. They accept any food. Put the pregnant female in a separate small tank, from which she should be removed after giving birth to be on the afe side, although she does not usually eat the young ones.

Echinodorus quadricostatus FASSETT

This plant belongs to the family Alismataceae. There are three varieties altogether of which only *E. quadricostatus* var. *xinguensis* from the central and lower reaches of the Amazon and its tributaries (Rio Xingu), is grown in the aquarium. The aquarist usually knows it under the incorrect name, *Echinodorus intermedius*.

The plant forms a rosette of leaves almost without petiole, narrow, lanceolate, bright green, 10—15 cms (4—6 ins) long and 1 cm. ($\frac{1}{2}$ in.) wide. In gloomier tanks the plants are taller and richer, in well-lit ones leaves are usually short.

This plant can be grown in any environment, in the front of the bottom part of the aquarium. It propagates quickly from rootstock offshoots and forms light green growths.

100

Poecilia (Mollienesia) velifera REGAN

Sail-fin Molly

This fish of the family Poeciliidae originates in the Yucatan peninsula.

The body of these live-born fishes is relatively large and stout, elongated, slightly compressed, shiny blue with a blue-green mesh-like pattern and with dense rows of glistening blue dots. On the throat and breast they are usually bluish-green and sometimes orange. The dorsal and caudal fins are embellished with a pearly sheen. The male is identified by its more developed fins and an inseminating organ called a gonopodium.

In the aquarium this fish degenerates badly and does not reach the usual body or fin size indicated by imported samples. This is caused by breeding fishes in small tanks with a lack of plant food. They should be bred and procreated in the same way as other live-born fishes, the only difference being that the temperature should not fall below 24°C (75°F).

Echinodorus berteroi (SPRENG.) FASSETT

Cellophane Plant

This plant belongs to the family Alismataceae and comes from the southern parts of the U.S.A., from Central America and the West Indies.

The submersed leaves are of various shapes, ranging from spiky, lanceolate, and egg-shaped, to a broad heart-shaped. They are light green, transparent, and very fragile. In good conditions floating or emersed leaves are sometimes formed. Each plant has between ten and thirty leaves, of which nearly every one is shaped differently. No wonder this is considered one of the most beautiful plants.

It is grown in a very poor bed to prevent the formation of emersed leaves. It is not particular as to temperature, but prefers soft water.

It is propagated primarily through seeds which is the main reason that the plant is not very plentiful in aquaria.

Polycentrus schomburgki MÜLLER ET TROSCHEL

South American Leaf-fish

This fish belongs to the family Nandidae and comes from the Amazon tributaries, west Guyana, and Trinidad. It was introduced into Europe in 1907.

The body of the fish is rotund, deep, up to 7 cms (3 ins) long, the basic colouring fluctuating according to its mood, the temperature, and the colouring of the bed. The most common colouring is grey-brown to grey-black with black, silvery, shiny dots and flecks. From the eye to the snout there are three dark yellow-edged, wedge-shaped bands. It has a protrusible mouth with teeth. The male is darker and bigger and during the spawning season turns completely black.

They should be bred apart from other fishes or in the company of fishes of the same size. They hide during the day and swim about only in the evening. A suitable temperature for them is 22°C (72°F). They love secluded places made of stones and will only accept live food.

They spawn at a temperature of 26°C (79°F). The female lays spawn on the underside of plant leaves, which the male then inseminates and subsequently looks after. The fry swim away after eight days and accept only fine live food.

Alternanthera reineckii BRIG.

This plant belongs to the family Amaranthaceae and comes from the tropical regions of South America. It was imported into Europe where it is usually sold under the trade name, *Telanthera osiris*.

It is smaller than other cultivated plants. Its leaves are green to olive-green on the upper side, red-brown or brown-green on the underside; they are not as distinctly coloured as other species. Under water it grows very well and quickly.

It should be grown in soft or medium-hard water, either in light or half-shade. It endures quite low temperatures (to 18°C; 64°F) and in the emersed form it flowers very easily. It is unsuitable for shallow tanks for then the tops of the plants grow out of the water, flower, and the lower leaves usually fall away.

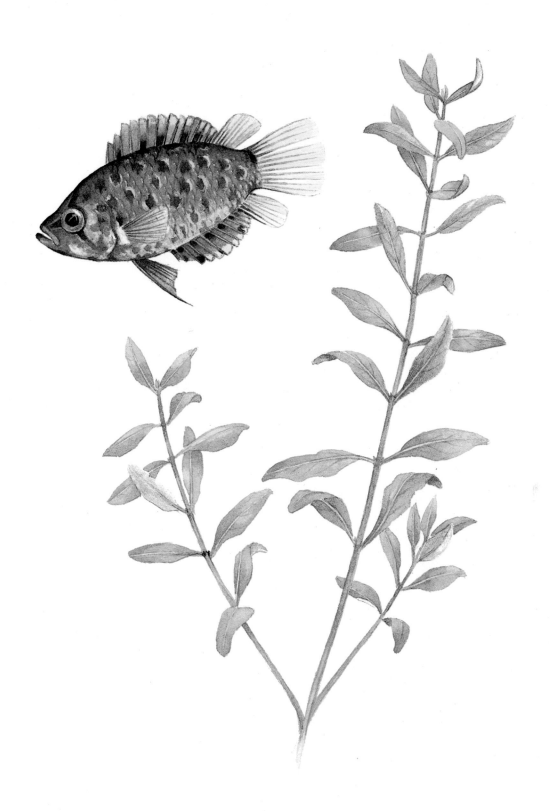

Pterophyllum scalare LICHTENSTEIN

Angel Fish, Scalare

This fish is a member of the family Cichlidae and it comes from the central reaches of the Amazon and its tributaries. It was imported into Europe in 1924. It produces a range of colourful mutations out of which the best known was described by Ahl and named *Pterophyllum eimekei*.

The body is very deep, strongly compressed, up to 12 cms (5 ins) long and 22 cms (9 ins) deep, silvery with a bluish sheen. The characteristic shape of the fish is formed mainly by fins of which the dorsal and ventral fins are sail shaped; the ventral fins are fibrous. On its sides there are five to seven transverse black stripes. The sex can be determined in the spawning season by the egg-laying organ of the female.

They should be bred in a large tank with deep water at a temperature of 22—24°C (72—75°F). They are quiet, peaceful, and require live food.

They procreate in a joint tank. The female lays spawn on a cleaned tough leaf and the male at the same time inseminates it. Then the leaf with the spawn should be cut away and put in another tank with similar water. Parental care can be replaced by aeration. The fry swim about on the sixth day and accept fine live food.

Echinodorus bleheri RATAJ

Amazon Swordplant

This plant belongs to the family Alismataceae but its origin is unknown. At present it comes from artificial nurseries in South America and Asia. It was formerly known under the incorrect names *E. paniculatus*, *E. rangeri*, or *E. tocatins*.

It is similar to *E. amazonicus* but its leaves are much broader and the petiole is not arched backwards like a sword. One plant alone forms a very rich clump consisting of twenty to thirty leaves reaching a length of 20—40 cms (8—16 ins) and a width of 4—6 cms (1½—2½ ins).

This *Echinodorus* is usually grown in a spacious tank with a poor bed. It is numbered amongst the most favourite species. The flower stalks form under water, and in their circular groups young plants are developed which can be separated after the formation of roots and replanted.

Symphysodon aequifasciata axelrodi SCHULTZ

Brown Discus, Yellow-brown Discus

This fish belongs to the family Cichlidae and comes from the watershed of the Amazon and the Rio Negro. It was imported into Europe in 1921 as *S. discus*.

The body is ·circular like a discus, well-flattened, up to 18 cms (7 ins) long, yellow-brown to red-brown with nine transverse bars. The sex of the fishes can be determined in the spawning season for the male has a pointed and the female a blunt cone-shaped sex organ. When the spawning season is over the male differs from the female in the colouring of its ventral fins. The male's red ventral fins have three oblong green bars while the female's fins have only one. They are bred like *Pterophyllum* but they require a higher temperature of about 25°C (77°F).

For procreation the temperature must be about 28°C (82°F), the water must be very soft and slightly acidic. When the fry start swimming about they obtain nourishment from the skin of their parents to which they adhere. The parents alternate in looking after the fry, and they can be removed only when the fry start accepting food by themselves.

Echinodorus amazonicus RATAJ

Small-leaved Amazon Swordplant

This plant belongs to the family Alismataceae and comes from the watershed of the central and lower reaches of the Amazon. It was reared for a long time under the incorrect name of *E. brevipedicellatus*.

The blades are long-lanceolate, longer than the petiole itself, green and arched backwards. The leaf measures 30—50 cms (12—20 ins). The flower stalk is thin and if it grows above the surface it develops four to nine white flowers in whorls, each flower about 1 cm. ($\frac{1}{2}$ in.) across. Usually the stalk remains submersed, then instead of flowers new plants form in the whorls, which root quickly.

Echinodorus amazonicus is planted in large tanks with medium-hard to soft water with an established bed. It is one of the most popular plants, especially suitable for fishes which lay their spawn on firm leaves. It propagates by creating young plants on the flower stalks.

108

Xiphophorus helleri HECKEL

Mexican Swordtail

This fish belongs to the family Cyprinodontidae and comes from southern Mexico, Guatemala, and Honduras. It was imported into Europe in 1909.

The body is slim and elongate, about 10 cms (4 ins) long, greenish, with red longitudinal stripes. The lower rays of the caudal fin are transformed into a long swordlike growth which is green or golden-red, lined in black at the top and bottom. Many colourful varieties have been reared, in green, red, golden, speckled and black.

Rearing and breeding are the same as with other live-born fishes. If there are more fishes in the tank, filtration and aeration are necessary. The pregnancy of the female varies from four to six weeks according to the temperature. The female lays eggs containing completely developed fishes which after leaving the mother's body break the membrane of the eggs and swim off.

Ceratophyllum submersum L.

Horn Worth

This plant belongs to the family Ceratophyllaceae and is found nearly all over the world.

It is a submersed plant which reaches the surface only with its uppermost parts. The leaves, arranged in whorls, are divided into fork-like shapes and have sharp teeth which are reminiscent of horns. The plants are hardy and winter well even in the cold. Genuine roots are missing and are replaced by short rhizoids.

It should be planted unrooted, floating freely in the water. It grows well in both cold and warm water, and can tolerate both soft and hard water. It requires plenty of light.

It is propagated by separating individual sections of the stem which then continue to grow.

Xiphophorus helleri 'Simpson' HECKEL

Simpson's Swordtail

This form was bred by the Simpson family in California in 1960. It is red with surprisingly elongated fins. The dorsal and the caudal fins are unusually beautiful.

Najas microdon A. BRAUN

This plant of the family Najadaceae comes from America. It is found from Nebraska in the U.S.A., across Central America, Venezuela, and Guyana to Uruguay and Argentina.

In cold climates it is an annual, while in the tropics it is perennial. The stems are delicate and grow in a mass of forklike twigs up to 1 m ($3\frac{1}{4}$ ft) long. The leaves are striped, green, bordered with fine teeth about 2.5 cms (1 in.) long and 1.5 cms ($\frac{3}{4}$ in.) wide.

Najas microdon is completely indifferent as to the water. It requires plenty of light and at a temperature of 20°C (68°F) it grows so quickly that it forms dense impenetrable clusters which can spread like weeds over the whole aquarium. As the stems are delicate they become broken when picked up and new plants grow. It is almost impossible to remove this plant completely from the aquarium. *Najas microdon* is suitable for spawning tanks.

112

Xiphophorus maculatus GÜNTHER

Red Swordtail, Moon Fish

This fish belongs to the family Cyprinodontidae and comes from eastern Mexico and Guatemala. It was imported into Europe in 1907.

The body is short, thick-set, slightly flattened, up to 5 cms (2 ins) long. The colour of this swordtail is very variable. By gradual crossbreeding the aquarist has produced a great number of colourful varieties in black, red, blue, yellow, golden, or variously flecked. The male is smaller, thinner and has a gonopodium.

They are bred in the same way as other live-born fishes and they procreate in the same manner.

Echinodorus tenellus (MART.) BUCH.

This plant belongs to the family Alismataceae and comes from a region extending from the southern states of the U.S.A. to central Brazil.

It is the smallest species of the genus *Echinodorus*, reaching an under-water height of only 3—5 cms ($1\frac{1}{4}$—2 ins). The leaves have fine spikes, usually only 2 mms ($\frac{1}{12}$ in.) wide, almost without petioles, and bright green.

They can be grown in any water at a temperature of 15—25°C (59—77°F) in a well-lit place. This is a plant ideally suited to being planted in the front part of the aquarium which it covers with a bright green, fine carpet. It propagates very quickly from rootstock spurs.

AFRICA

Aphyosemion arnoldi BOULENGER

Arnold's Lyretail, Aphyosemion

This fish belongs to the family Cyprinodontidae and comes from the Niger delta in Africa, from where it was first imported in 1905.

The body is pike-like, slim, up to 6.5 cms (2½ ins) long, olive-green with a black-brown back. On the whole body there are red flecks and dashes; the fins are very gaily coloured. The female is a drab brown with red dots and dashes, and lacks the gay colouring of the male's fins.

They should be bred in a small tank on their own at 20°C (68°F). They bite and are voracious. They love the shade and require stale water, which should be slightly acidic, pellucid, and slightly salty.

The fishes spawn in the same environment at 24°C (74°F). The female lays eggs on a soft bed (the most suitable is boiled peat). The pair press close together and the male buries the released spawn in the bed with a sharp blow of his tail. After spawning the parents should be removed and a little water left in the tank. The tank should then be put in the dark for fourteen to twenty days at a temperature of about 20°C (68°F). Then drain all the water from the peat, leave it to dry out slightly, put it in a bowl, cover it with glass, and leave it for a futher fourteen days. Then pour rain water on to the peat and at a temperature of 22°C (73°F) the fry hatch out in the course of several hours.

Anubias lanceolata SCHOTT.

African Spearblade

This plant belongs to the family Araceae and comes from Nigeria, Cameroun, and Gabon.

It is the most widely cultivated species of this genus. The leaf measures 30—35 cms (12—14 ins), of which about half consists of the blade, which is 15—20 cms (6—8 ins) long and about 5 cms (2 ins) wide. It is grown like cryptocorynes in a shady place, in soft, slightly acidic water with an established bed. In order to form a well-developed rootstock it needs a layer of sand on the bottom 10—15 cms (4—6 ins) deep.

It propagates in the same way as other species by subdivision of the rootstock.

Aphyosemion australe australe RACHOW

Cape Lopez Lyretail, Aphyosemion

This fish belongs to the family Cyprinodontidae and comes from Gabon in West Africa. It was imported into Europe in 1913.

The body is pike-like, brown-red, up to 6 cms (2½ ins) long. The gills and the front are embellished with green and blue flecks and stripes; the rest of the body and fins are covered with red dots and dashes. The male has elongated and very gaily coloured fins. The female is light brown with isolated red dots.

The fish should be bred in pellucid water without infusoria. They are peaceful and therefore it is possible to rear them with other quiet fishes of the same genus.

They procreate at a temperature of 24°C (75°F). They spawn on to floating roots or fine-leaved plants at several days interval. The spawn is strikingly large and clings to the plants. After spawning suck them away by means of a glass tube and keep them in the original water in a shallow bowl. The fry hatch out in about ten days and mature in ten weeks.

Anubias sp.

This plant belongs to the family Araceae and has not yet been reliably identified. It differs from other species cultivated in aquaria in having wavy-edged leaves. It grows to a height of 15—18 cms (6—7 ins) and so it is one of the medium-large sorts.

It is planted like other species. It grows very well under water and in mud and of all types it flowers the most easily and forms germinating seeds. The white and slightly yellowish flowers are in a green spathe tube.

It is propagated by dividing the rootstock or by seeds.

Aphyosemion bivittatum bivittatum LÖNNBERG

Red Lyretail, Aphyosemion

This fish belongs to the family Cyprinodontidae and comes from Cameroun and the Niger delta. It was imported into Europe in 1908.

The body is pike-like, up to 6 cms ($2\frac{1}{2}$ ins) long, red-brown, and lighter towards the stomach. There are two distinct longitudinal, brown to blue-black bands along the whole body. The fins are very gaily coloured, the males' are noticeably longer. The female is distinctly coloured, smaller, and has rounded fins. They are reared in the same way as other related fishes. They usually live in the central part of the tank, and because they like to dart about it is necessary to cover the tank.

They procreate in the same way as other fishes of the genus *Aphyosemion*, but at spawning time the male is very aggressive and often kills the female. The fry mature in six months, but for spawning nine-month-old fishes should be used.

Ammania senegalensis LAM.

This plant is a member of the family Lythraceae and comes from the whole of the northern part of tropical Africa.

The stem is usually bent at the bottom, partly creeping, green, bare, about 3—5 mms ($\frac{1}{8}$—$\frac{1}{5}$ in.) thick. The leaves are without petiole, longitudinally oval, 2—4 cms ($\frac{3}{4}$—$1\frac{1}{2}$ ins) long and 0.8—1.5 cms ($\frac{1}{4}$—$\frac{1}{2}$ in.) wide, deep green, with the underside darker than the top surface.

They are grown in a poor bed, in a soft or medium-hard water in a well-lit place. They require light in winter otherwise they lose their bottom leaves and only the tops remain leafy.

It is propagated by rooting top cuttings, but this is only successful in spring and summer. The best plants are acquired from seeds which should be placed at the bottom of a tank 10—15 cms (4—6 ins) deep.

120

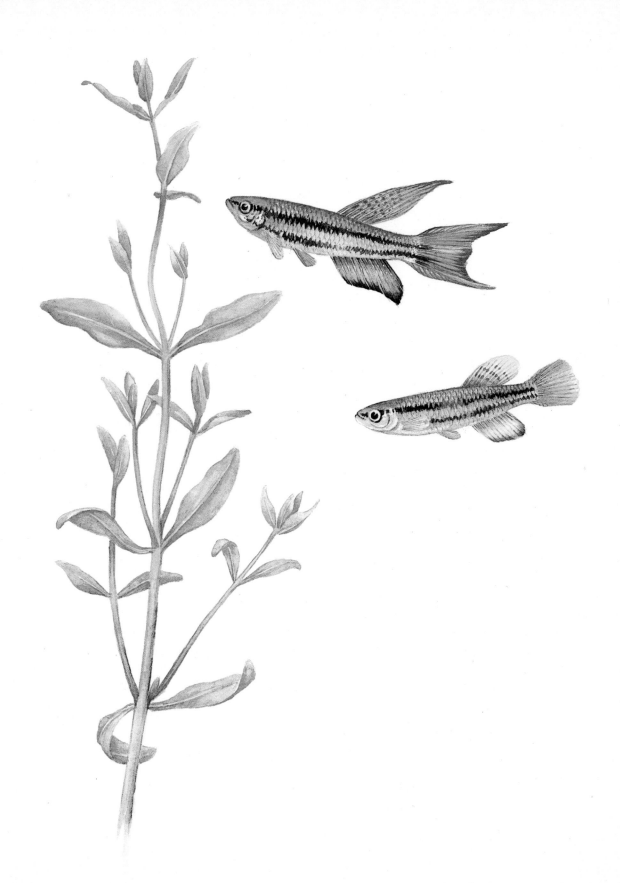

Bedotia geayi PELLEGRIN

This fish belongs to the family Atherinidae and comes from Madagascar. It was introduced into Europe in 1953.

The body is tall, elongate, strongly compressed, up to 12 cms (5 ins) long with two dorsal fins. A black longitudinal stripe stretches from the mouth backwards, widening and then narrowing again towards the caudal fin, the second stripe is grey-blue and is located on the bottom half of the body. The male usually has his caudal fin lined with red.

They should be reared in a large tank at a temperature of 22°C (72°F). They are peaceful and therefore suitable for a community tank. They procreate at 24°C (75°F) in well-oxygenated, slightly salted water. The spawn is deposited on to fine-leaved plants from which it is suspended by a short fibre. The fry hatch out in eight days and are not endangered by their parents.

Aponogeton fenestralis (POIR.) HOOK
Madagascar Lace Plant ·

This plant belongs to the family Aponogetonaceae and comes from Madagascar.

It has a cylindrical rootstock from which grow leaves up to 30 cms (12 ins) long with oval blades, rounded at the tips. The leaves resemble lace for the tissue between the veins breaks up and forms holes. The inflorescence consists of two or more spikes and measures 5—7 cms (2—3 ins).

It should be grown in a tank with very clean and very soft water, of which about a third should be changed for fresh or one to two days old rain water every fortnight in summer and every four weeks in winter. It usually does not survive in tanks with fishes so that it is necessary to replace the plants with imported bulbs. It is also possible to propagate it from seeds, but this is very difficult and aquarists are usually dependent on imports.

122

Epiplatys chaperi SAUVAGE
Fire-mouth Epiplatys

This fish belongs to the family Cyprinodontidae and comes from tropical western Africa, from Sierra Leone to Ghana. It was imported in 1908.

The body is pike-like, flattened at the top, up to 6 cms (2½ ins) long. The dorsal fin is placed relatively towards the back, the sides are greenish to blue, the stomach is yellowish. On the flanks there are five to seven transverse black bands. The female is smaller, indistinctly coloured and has rounded fins, while the male has them elongated in apices.

These fishes should be bred in a medium-sized tank at 20°C (68°F), in which the vegetation is completed by floating plants. They are peaceful, and usually live just under the surface of the water.

They procreate at 24°C (75°F). The females lay spawn on to the roots of floating plants and eventually on to fine-leaved plants. Spawning often lasts several weeks, therefore the clumps of plants with spawn are sometimes put into another tank. Then a fresh clump of plants is added, on to which spawning continues. It is recommended that several males are put with one female. The spawn and fry should be protected from the light. The fry hatch out in about ten days and stay near the water surface.

Anubias nana ENGLER

This plant belongs to the family Araceae and comes from Cameroun.

It is the smallest species of the genus and its leaves reach a length of 10—12 cms (4—5 ins) at the most. The blades are a little shorter than the petiole; they are egg-shaped and oval, on the upper side dark, shiny green, on the underside light green.

They should be grown in an established bed, in slightly acidic water in a dim light.

They are propagated by subdivision of their rootstock. Separate a several-years-old rootstock from the mother plant and either divide it according to the dormant rootlets and then leave them to rest for a while, or place the whole rootstock in water and divide it only when new plants form from the dormant rootlets.

124

Hemichromis bimaculatus GILL

Jewel-fish, Red Cichlid

This fish belongs to the family Cichlidae and comes from the watersheds of the Niger, Nile, and Congo. It was imported in 1907.

The body is elongate, greenish-yellow with a reddish tinge. On its gills and at the base of its tail there are darker flecks. But the colouring is variable. Sometimes it is red with shining rows of sky-blue dots on the sides, which even reach the gills and fins. The female is distinctly redder.

They should be bred in a large tank at 20°C (68°F), if possible separately. They are aggressive, and are therefore unsuitable companions for smaller fishes. They tear up the vegetation and so the tank should only be furnished with tough plants and the bottom should be covered with pebbles and large stones on to which the fishes spawn.

Crinum natans BAKER

This plant is a member of the family Amaryllidaceae and comes from tropical Africa. It has a bulb which measures 3—6 cms (1—2½ ins) and partly sticks out from the bed. The leaves form on a short stalk and they are crescent-shaped, with longitudinal veins, with straight or slightly wavy edges. They are 2—5 cms (¾—2 ins) wide and up to 1.5 m (5 ft) long, so that they grow at right angles to the surface and then they crawl just beneath it.

This *Crinum* thrives best at temperatures of 20—30°C (68—86°F) in a not too nutritious soil and in a well-lit place. It is one of the most valuable aquarium plants.

It propagates by bulbs which now and then form on the main bulb. Propagation in the aquarium is very slow.

126

Nothobranchius rachovi E. AHL

Rachow's Fundulus

This fish belongs to the family Cyprinodontidae and comes from eastern Africa. It was imported in 1925.

The body is pike-like, rather plump, up to 4.5 cms (2 ins) long. The sides of the male are blue-green covered with reddish gold, orange-yellow, and red flecks and dashes; the scales are edged with orange. Most of the fins are very colourful and elongated. The female is smaller, light-grey, with brownish fins.

They should be reared in a medium-sized tank at a temperature of 20°C (68°F). They are not particular, and only require soft and acidic water with a soft bed composed of boiled peat or fine sand. They are friendly towards other sorts of fishes, but the males often fight viciously among themselves.

The spawn take a long time to develop, often twenty to twenty-four weeks. The hatched-out fry should be fed with small live food.

Lagarosiphon muscoides HARVEY

This plant belongs to the family Hydrocharitaceae and comes from central and southern Africa. It is usually sold under the trade name, *Elodea crispa*.

It differs from plants of the genus *Elodea* in that the leaves are not in whorls but sit on the stems in dense spirals. They are medium to deep green, about 2 cms ($\frac{3}{4}$ in.) long, arched backwards, and with finely serrated margins.

It should be raised in the same conditions as other plants of the genus *Elodea*, but *Lagarosiphon muscoides* is rather more fastidious. It grows more slowly in acidic water, it thrives in medium to strong light and at temperatures of about 20°C (68°F). Because it absorbs considerable amounts of calcium salts, it makes hard water softer. It grows well in medium-hard tap water and it is one of the most pleasing plants. It propagates by stem segments rooting.

128

Pelmatochromis kribensis BOULENGER

This fish belongs to the family Cichlidae and comes from tropical West Africa and from the Niger delta. It was introduced in 1951.

The body is elongate, slightly compressed, up to 5 cms (2 ins) long, of very variable colouring. It is usually yellow-brown with a wide, brown, longitudinal stripe and a large wine-red fleck on both sides of the stomach. The fins are reddish. The male is bigger, slimmer, and has the top part of its caudal fin embellished with round dark flecks.

The fishes are bred in a large, well-stocked tank at 22—24°C (72—75°F). They are peaceful, sociable, and not fussy. Put an upturned flower-pot on the bed, for the fishes like to hide.

Spawning takes place in this hideaway. The female turns her stomach upwards during the laying of the eggs and then the male inseminates them. The fry are looked after by both parents.

Anubias congensis N. E. BROWN

This plant belongs to the family Araceae and comes from the Congo and Guinea.

It is the largest cultivated species with leaves up to 40 cms (16 ins) long. The blades measure 25×10—12 cms (10×4—5 ins); they are deep green with distinct veins on the top surface, while on the underside they are light green to greenish-white. They should be grown in a spacious tank with soft acidic water in a shady place. They form a large rootstock and therefore require a layer of sand at least 10—15 cms (4—6 ins) deep. The rootstock which is 5—15 cms (2—6 ins) long usually forms after several years and by its subdivision ten to fifteen young plants can be acquired, which at first develop very slowly. Development is quicker in mud. It is even possible to grow *Anubias* in flower-pots as a house plant.

List of illustrated species

132